De-internationalization and Re-internationalization of the Firm

"This is a very interesting and thought-provoking book. The authors highlight the continuing process of adjustment and re-adjustment of business structure and business strategy that is necessary for firms to survive and grow in a volatile and competitive global economy. The authors point out that firms must be prepared to internationalize, de-internationalize, and re-internationalize as circumstances dictate and recommend that business leaders adopt a business model innovation approach, which they discuss in an informative and accessible way. This is good news for the international business profession, and for business executives too, as it means that abstract theories and practitioner-oriented theories are converging on a common approach to contemporary issues in global business. This book is therefore to be welcomed, not only for its practical wisdom but also for its contribution to an evolving theoretical approach which can shed new light on the international business system as a whole."
—Mark Casson, Professor, *Department of Economics, University of Reading, and Henley Business School*

"As we witness the retreat of globalization in the current multipolar geopolitical context, it is critical researchers explore the many facets of multinational companies' cross-border activity. The book introduces a series of novel perspectives, such as deploying Business Model Innovation strategies and configuration frameworks to the subject at hand, removing the globalization bias from the de-internationalization discussion and treating this topic in a factual, objective manner that can deliver positive results to a firm undergoing the considerable challenges of operating in complex regulatory systems. The result is much-needed clarity and insight for both business operators and academics looking for a guiding light in the increasingly challenging international business environment."
—Mihai Pohontu, CEO, *Amber*

"Financial crimes are few of many reasons why firms withdraw from international markets or fail. Dealing with, fighting financial crimes in today's volatile, uncertain, and technology-driven landscape requires constant innovation. The intricate process of de-internationalization and re-internationalization of firms, as outlined in this book, provides a vital framework for understanding how businesses can adapt, survive, and thrive. By exploring business model innovation and its interdependent relation with international business, this publication offers critical insights for practitioners and policymakers navigating pan-national challenges. Its thorough analysis and practical frameworks will undoubtedly serve as a touchstone for both academic research and real-world applications that can be adapted inter alia to enhance firm cross-border strategies aimed at mitigating risks associated with financial crimes."

—Michal Gromek, Compliance Director, *G7 Research Group and Chair of the Digital Asset Task Force of the Global Coalition to Fight Financial Crime*

"In today's volatile, uncertain, complex and ambiguous world we witness and will continue to witness de-internationalization and re-internationalization of small and large firms. A decision to withdraw from a market or several markets can be a difficult one, sometimes painful. Going back into the "game," to re-internationalize, can be also a brave choice, especially when it follows an unsuccessful internationalization. Such decisions shall be supported by Business Model Innovation, a key to a successful de-internationalization and re-internationalization. Scholars and practitioners will enjoy this book in which the authors present original interdisciplinary frameworks to assist firms in their internationalization, de-internationalization, and re-internationalization efforts supported by Business Model Innovation."

—Humphrey Lau, CEO, *DESMI*

Jesper Chrautwald Sort
Yariv Taran • Romeo V. Turcan

De-internationalization and Re-internationalization of the Firm

Business Model Innovation for Growth and Survival

A foreword by Mark Casson

Jesper Chrautwald Sort
AAU Business School
Aalborg University
Aalborg, Denmark

Yariv Taran
AAU Business School
Aalborg University
Aalborg, Denmark

Romeo V. Turcan
AAU Business School
Aalborg University
Aalborg, Denmark

ISBN 978-3-031-81773-1   ISBN 978-3-031-81774-8 (eBook)
https://doi.org/10.1007/978-3-031-81774-8

© The Editor(s) (if applicable) and The Author(s), under exclusive license to Springer Nature Switzerland AG 2025

This work is subject to copyright. All rights are solely and exclusively licensed by the Publisher, whether the whole or part of the material is concerned, specifically the rights of translation, reprinting, reuse of illustrations, recitation, broadcasting, reproduction on microfilms or in any other physical way, and transmission or information storage and retrieval, electronic adaptation, computer software, or by similar or dissimilar methodology now known or hereafter developed.

The use of general descriptive names, registered names, trademarks, service marks, etc. in this publication does not imply, even in the absence of a specific statement, that such names are exempt from the relevant protective laws and regulations and therefore free for general use.

The publisher, the authors and the editors are safe to assume that the advice and information in this book are believed to be true and accurate at the date of publication. Neither the publisher nor the authors or the editors give a warranty, expressed or implied, with respect to the material contained herein or for any errors or omissions that may have been made. The publisher remains neutral with regard to jurisdictional claims in published maps and institutional affiliations.

This Palgrave Macmillan imprint is published by the registered company Springer Nature Switzerland AG.
The registered company address is: Gewerbestrasse 11, 6330 Cham, Switzerland

If disposing of this product, please recycle the paper.

To our families for their continuous support and belief in what we are doing...

Foreword

This is a very interesting and thought-provoking book. The authors highlight the continuing process of adjustment and re-adjustment of business structure and business strategy that is necessary for firms to survive and grow in a volatile and competitive global economy. The authors recommend that business leaders adopt a business model innovation approach, which they discuss in an informative and accessible way.

The authors point out that firms must be prepared to internationalize, de-internationalize, and re-internationalize as circumstances dictate. It is no longer appropriate, as in the early post-war period, to regard internationalization as a signal of success and de-internationalization as a signal of failure. De-internationalization may well be a prudent response when political frictions, exhaustion of resources, and rising costs render existing international operations untenable. The global economy has always been volatile to some degree, but recently, environmental change, social pressures, and increasing political conflict (which are all connected) have led to a rapid increase in volatility. The modern economy is, regrettably, becoming as volatile as it was in the inter-war period.

These challenges to globalization are likely to impact not only the location of production and sales, but also the contractual arrangements used to coordinate them. In some cases, vertical integration may be strengthened to exclude external rivals from access to strategic resources, while in other cases it may be weakened in order to reduce dependence on internal resources and procure resources in a more flexible way. Similarly horizontal integration may be reduced to make better use of the expertise of independent, expatriate-owned firms that may possess better knowledge of local conditions in foreign markets.

My own background is in the economics of international business and, in particular, the models and methods that are employed by economists to analyze trends in the global economy. It might be thought that there is little connection between the two approaches, but in fact, they are closely aligned. Economists are beginning to recognize that global markets are segmented and that products traded internationally are often differentiated to meet the needs of specific segments of that market. In this context, coordination of the global economy is affected by a set of potential links between different sources of demand and different sources of supply; unlike Alfred Marshall's classic theory of the market, however, not every supplier is in contact with every customer; each customer segment can be supplied only by a subset of producers, and each producer can supply only a subset of customers. When modeled in a suitable way, the equilibrium outcomes are relatively easy to solve, and it aligns very well with the implications of the BMI approach adopted in this book. This is good news for the international business profession and for business executives, too, as it means that abstract theories and practitioner-oriented theories are converging on a common approach to contemporary issues in global business. This book is therefore to be welcomed, not only for its practical wisdom but also for its contribution to an evolving theoretical approach which can shed new light on the international business system, as a whole.

Department of Economics, University of Reading, and Henley Business School Reading, UK

Mark Casson

Preface

It's easier to see both sides of a question than the answer.—Arnold Glasow

We started "consiliencing" just over seven years ago. Frustrations and opportunities led us to "jump together" and to this book. We observed then that the two disciplines or the "two cultures" we come from—business model and international business—were reluctant to talk to each other, to converse. Each discipline has its own reasons for this "alienation." Business model is a young, embryonic discipline in its yet formative years to become a well-established and respected discipline. Since its inception, it may have become closed and over-protective of its newly developed concepts and frameworks, keeping at bay the "outsiders" and resisting borrowing from other disciplines to advance its own. International business, on the other hand, may see itself as a mature discipline with well-established, one may say beautiful and elegant, theories that can predict quite accurately firms' behaviors. At the same, it might be a discipline in crisis of new ideas but eager to "look over" and borrow from other disciplines. But when you cannot get in, there is not much you can learn. Despite all this, attempts have been made by international business researchers to research business models *and* business model innovation, but seldom "on par."

At the same time, this lack of consilience and alienation between the two cultures, as well as their diverse and divergent logics, as defined by respective constitutive assumptions (paradigms), epistemological stances (metaphors), and favored methodologies (puzzle solving), pointed to academic, practice, and policy opportunities to bring these two disciplines together and contribute to a better understanding of firms' nonlinear cross-border activities and overall growth. We identified some of the opportunities in 2018 and have been "consiliencing" since then. This book is a result of our interdisciplinary "jumping together."

Of the three core components that form the international business or cross-border activity of the firm—internationalization, de-internatio nalization, and re-internationalization—the most researched and understood is the first. Continuous weighty de-globalization and de-internationalization of firms, global value chains, sectors and states, that has increased in recent years, made academia, practice, and policy take notice and try to understand and study it. Compared to internationalization and de-internationalization, re-internationalization is less understood and researched and is yet to be studied systematically, including its relationship with de-internationalization. It was at this juncture that we spotted an opportunity to explore this relationship through business model lenses, conjecturing that the relationship between de-internationalization and re-internationalization is best understood, theoretically and empirically, through the moderating effect of business model innovation.

This book is centered on this conjecture, which we explore theoretically. Initially, we try understanding de-internationalization and re-internationalization separately, through business model innovation lenses, and then conceptualize their relationship through the moderating effect of business model innovation. This led us to the development of the international business-business model research program. The program is conceptualized as the intersection of the core dimensions of these two disciplines, international business: internationalization, de-internation alization and re-internationalization and business model innovation: value proposition, value segment, value configuration, value network, and value capture. In addition to its international and interdisciplinary natures, this research program will also be inter-technological and inter-sectorial.

Despite the complexity of the international business-business model intersection and challenges that lie ahead, we believe future research at the intersection of these two research streams and cultures will contribute to a better understanding of firms' nonlinear cross-border activities that are currently under-researched. We also believe this international business-business model research program will have impacts on academia, practice, and policy through a better understanding of how firms can reconfigure or reinvent their business models during failure, growth, decline, or (strategic) departure from what is normal or expected. Such an embryonic research program will undoubtedly result in more questions than answers, making it an exciting, thought-provoking avenue for future research and practice in a volatile, uncertain, complex, and ambiguous world.

We wish to express our appreciation and thanks to the Palgrave Pivot team for their guidance and support. We thank Cambridge Proofreading & Editing for improving the flow of the work and ensuring clarity throughout the book.

Aalborg, Denmark

Jesper Chrautwald Sort
Yariv Taran
Romeo V. Turcan

Contents

1 **Introduction** 1
   1.1 *Sailing Through Troubled Waters* 1
   1.2 *Aim and Approach* 3
   1.3 *Book Structure* 6
   References 9

2 **Internationalization** 13
   2.1 *Setting the Compass for an Unknown Adventure* 13
   2.2 *Process and State* 14
   2.3 *Gradual Or Instant* 14
   2.4 *Crossing National Borders* 17
   2.5 *Commitment* 18
   2.6 *Context* 19
   2.7 *Concluding Remarks* 19
   References 21

3 **De-internationalization** 27
   3.1 *Swimming Toward Calm Waters* 27
   3.2 *Defining De-internationalization* 28
      3.2.1 *Taken for Granted* 28
      3.2.2 *Understanding Its Key Concerns* 29
      3.2.3 *Constructing Its Domain* 31
   3.3 *The "whys" of De-internationalization* 35
   3.4 *The "hows" of De-internationalization* 36

	3.5 Special Cases of De-internationalization	38
	3.6 Concluding Remarks	40
	References	47

4 Re-internationalization — 53
    4.1 Re-calibrating the Compass, the Ship — 53
    4.2 Linking Re-internationalization to De-internationalization and Internationalization — 54
    4.3 Defining Re-internationalization — 61
    4.4 The "whys" of Re-internationalization — 63
    4.5 The "hows" of Re-internationalization — 64
    4.6 Concluding Remarks — 66
    References — 68

5 Business Model Innovation — 71
    5.1 Weathering the Storm — 71
    5.2 Defining BMI — 72
        5.2.1 BMI Types — 72
        5.2.2 Zooming-in and Zooming-out — 75
    5.3 BM Configurations and the 5-V Framework — 78
    5.4 Concluding Remarks — 80
    References — 83

6 BMI and De-internationalization — 87
    6.1 Anchoring in Calm Waters — 87
    6.2 The "hows" of De-internationalization and BM Value Drivers — 89
    6.3 The "whys" of De-internationalization and BM Value Drivers — 92
        6.3.1 Linking the "whys" of De-internationalization to Value Proposition — 94
        6.3.2 Linking the "whys" of De-internationalization to Value Segment — 95
        6.3.3 Linking the "whys" of De-internationalization to Value Configuration — 96
        6.3.4 Linking the "whys" of De-internationalization to Value Network — 97

	6.3.5 Linking the "whys" of De-internationalization to Value Capture	98
6.4	Concluding Remarks	99
References		100

7 BMI and Re-internationalization — 103
7.1 Setting a New Voyage — 103
7.2 The "hows" of Re-internationalization and BMI Types — 104
7.3 The "whys" of Re-internationalization and BM Value Drivers — 106
    7.3.1 Linking the "whys" of Re-internationalization to Value Proposition — 106
    7.3.2 Linking the "whys" of Re-internationalization to Value Segment — 106
    7.3.3 Linking the "whys" of Re-internationalization to Value Configuration — 108
    7.3.4 Linking the "whys" of Re-internationalization to Value Network — 109
    7.3.5 Linking the "whys" of Re-internationalization to Value Capture — 111
7.4 A First Step Toward an IB-BM Framework — 112
7.5 Concluding Remarks — 115
References — 116

8 Toward an IB-BM Research Program — 117
8.1 Captain's Log — 117
8.2 Substantive (Inter)disciplinary Contributions — 118
8.3 Toward an IB-BM Research Program — 119
    8.3.1 IB-BM Research Program Framework — 119
    8.3.2 IB-BM Research Sub-Programs — 121
    8.3.3 A multidimensional and Multilevel Research Program — 123
8.4 An Exciting "voyage" Ahead — 124
References — 126

Index — 127

About the Authors

Jesper Chrautwald Sort is an associate professor at the Aalborg University Business School in Denmark. His research interest lies at the intersection of management accounting, business models, and entrepreneurship, with a focus on understanding and improving management accounting and performance management in SMEs, inspired by business model innovation. Jesper led series of initiatives in the Danish investment community, including capacity building in the local government on the investment process between entrepreneurs and investors, such as business angels, lean start-ups, and business model innovation, in particular, and investment processes, in general. This academic-practice-policy experience and collaboration informed the development of innovative, problem-based teaching and learning methods. Jesper received his BSc in Business Economics, MSc in Management Accounting, and PhD in Entrepreneurial Finance from Aalborg University.

Yariv Taran is an associate professor at Aalborg University Business School in Denmark, specializing in the management of risk and uncertainty in business model innovation processes. His research interests also include decision-making, entrepreneurship, and sustainability. His work has been published in several international journals, including *Decision Sciences*, *International Journal of Operations & Production Management*, *Technology Analysis & Strategic Management*, and *European Journal of Innovation Management*. He is the lead author of the book *The Business Model Innovation Process: Preparation, Organization, and Management*, published by Routledge. Yariv holds a BSc in Management and Sociology from the Open University of Israel, an MSc in Economics and Business Administration, and a PhD in Business Model Innovation from Aalborg University.

Romeo V. Turcan is a professor at the Aalborg University Business School in Denmark, an adjunct professor at the Trinity College Dublin in Ireland, and a visiting professor at the University of Cambridge in the United Kingdom. Romeo's main research interests include de-internationalization and de-globalization, high-impact international entrepreneurship, legitimation of newness, and theory building across diverse disciplines and contexts. Romeo is the founder and coordinator of an interdisciplinary collaborative research program, the Theory Building Research Programme (http://www.tbrp.aau.dk). Prior to commencing his academic career, Romeo served in a range of positions involving public policy intervention in the restructuring, rationalization, and modernization of both the private and public sectors, including the energy, military, management consulting, ICT, and higher education sectors. He founded and served as the CEO of a branch of an international NGO. Romeo has led five EU-funded projects with a total value of approximately €8 million. Romeo obtained his mechanical engineering diploma from the Air Force Engineering Military Academy in Riga, Latvia, and post-graduate diploma in Philology from the Moldova State University in Chisinau. He obtained his MSc and PhD from the University of Strathclyde's Marketing Department and Hunter Centre for Entrepreneurship, respectively, in Glasgow.

List of Figures

Fig. 1.1	A relationship between cross-border activity and BMI	4
Fig. 1.2	De-internationalization, re-internationalization, and BMI intersection framework	4
Fig. 3.1	De-internationalization as a turning point	32
Fig. 3.2	The typology of de-internationalization	34
Fig. 3.3	The "hows" of de-internationalization	37
Fig. 4.1	From liquidation to resurrection to re-internationalization	58
Fig. 4.2	The typology of re-internationalization	66
Fig. 8.1	IB-BM research program framework	120
Fig. 8.2	A re-internationalization sub-program: An example	122
Fig. 8.3	Researching IB-BM intersection at micro, meso, and macro levels	123

List of Tables

Table 3.1	The "whys" of de-internationalization	35
Table 3.2	De-internationalization of universities	41
Table 6.1	De-internationalization "hows" and BM value drivers	90
Table 6.2	The "whys" of de-internationalization and BM value drivers	93
Table 7.1	Foreign market (re-)entry modes and BMI	104
Table 7.2	Evaluating re-internationalization postures	110
Table 7.3	A first step toward an IB-BM framework	112

List of Vignette

Vignette 2.1	Nike—Diversified market entry modes strategy	15
Vignette 2.2	Jolla—Re-born global	16
Vignette 2.3	Procter & Gamble—Dual growth strategy of retrenchment and expansion	17
Vignette 3.1	A sameness of internationalization and de-internationalization reasons	31
Vignette 3.2	De-internationalization of firms from Russia	39
Vignette 4.1	De-internationalization and re-internationalization of General Motors	55
Vignette 4.2	Phoenix-rising-from-the-ashes re-internationalization	58
Vignette 5.1	Open innovation at LEGO	73
Vignette 5.2	Zooming-in and zooming-out at Alpha	76
Vignette 5.3	5-V framework at Spotify	79
Vignette 6.1	International market exit—misaligned value perception	94
Vignette 6.2	International market exit—challenges in achieving economies of scale	96
Vignette 6.3	Navigating market exit: pricing challenges in international markets	98
Vignette 7.1	From failure to success: Effecting re-internationalization	107
Vignette 7.2	There is always a way to re-internationalize	109

CHAPTER 1

Introduction

The world is full of thorns and thistles. It's all in how you grasp them.
—Arnold Glasow

1.1 Sailing Through Troubled Waters

We live in a volatile, uncertain, complex, and ambiguous (VUCA) world, which can no longer be described as stable, certain, simple, and concrete. Individual choices, institutions, routines, fears, power, politics, collective action, long-term thinking, free will, conformity, and legitimation, to name a few, are in a fluid state.[1] The ways and forms of organizing

> structures that limit individual choices, institutions that guard repetitions of routines, patterns of acceptable behavior can no longer and are not expected to keep their shape for long, because they decompose and melt faster than the time it takes to cast them, and once they are cast, for them to set.[2]

It is more difficult than ever to manage a business in such a VUCA world, where "predictable unpredictability is not going away."[3] Future economic trends and market changes are uncertain. Product lifecycles, strategic choices, capabilities, and routines have become shorter than before, and innovation is increasingly externalized.

Cross-border activities of a firm add additional VUCA challenges and issues. From an international business (IB) perspective, cross-border *pattern and capacity* and *logic* are constantly threatened globally, internationally, and domestically. Decision-makers regularly assess the suitability of their firm's cross-border patterns, whether exporting, franchising, licensing, joint ventures, acquisitions, or green or brownfield investments, aiming to address *how, why, when, what, where,* and *who* regarding their product and/or service portfolio mix, timing, pace, and direction of cross-border activities.[5] They also relentlessly review and reconfigure their firm's cross-border capacity, as defined by the resource and capability base (e.g., technological, human, and financial) of the firm, cross-border strategy, organizational structure and processes, relationships, innovation postures, experience, and motivations to operate internationally.[6]

Extant empirical evidence suggests that in a VUCA world, firms withdraw in abundance from international markets or de-internationalize,[7] and very few re-internationalize.[8] Given its high relevance to practitioners and policymakers, firms' nonlinear processes of cross-border activities through various de-internationalization and re-internationalization cycles and waves should be conceptually and empirically developed and understood.[9] Compared to internationalization, de-internationalization has been less researched and is a less understood phenomenon,[10] and re-internationalization has yet to be studied systematically.[11]

Since the earlier conceptualization of de-internationalization[12] and recent interest in re-internationalization, theory building within these phenomena remains scarce. Access to data is one of the reasons why de-internationalization and associated re-internationalization are under-researched, as the former is largely seen as negative, undesirable,[13] and often perceived as failure[14]—after all, who wants to admit failure, let alone "brag" about it. Given the negative, undesirable features of de-internationalization, a researcher would get from their respondents *vague data* (when respondents deliberately evade revealing key issues), *proper-lined data* (when respondents tell the official policy rather than what is really happening), or *zero data* (when respondents tell, reveal nothing at all).[15] Exploring re-internationalization without exploring and understanding de-internationalization will not give the researcher a full picture of a firm's cross-border activity.

Another reason why de-internationalization and re-internationalization are under-researched is the extant misconceptions, including semantic and theoretical, in defining and positioning de-internationalization and re-internationalization within the IB field.[16] For example, there is a tendency among IB scholars to position internationalization, de-internationalization, and re-internationalization as part of internationalization. Such an erroneous approach to positioning de-internationalization and re-internationalization within IB limits the study of de-internationalization and re-internationalization. This inaccurate approach manifests especially when IB researchers employ IB theories, frameworks, and concepts that explain internationalization, that is, using a *linear, forward-looking process*, to study de-internationalization and re-internationalization, which are *nonlinear, multidirectional* processes.[17]

In this book, we position "*internationalization, de-internationalization, and re-internationalization*" as part of the "*cross-border activity*" of a firm.[18] Two more reasons to mention: the limited scope of IB theories to explain the nonlinear behavior of firms, such as de-internationalization and re-internationalization, especially in a VUCA world; and IB scholars' general reluctance to leave their "comfort zones" and "dive" into other disciplines to borrow new, diverse and divergent, ideas, theories, and concepts. After all, innovation and progress emerge when new, diverse ideas, theories, and concepts collide.[19]

We draw on the business model innovation (BMI) framework to develop a better understanding of the nonlinear cross-border behavior of firms. We *conjecture that the relationship between de-internationalization and re-internationalization is best understood, theoretically and empirically, through a moderating effect of business model innovation* (Fig. 1.1).[20] BMI, as an emerging framework, aims to explain the success and failures of the firm[21] and how it can adapt to and/or innovate in new internal and/or external settings and circumstances.[22] Complexity, uncertainty, and risks, coupled with radical and more disruptive BMI, have become quintessential in today's competitive landscape and are likely to define and pervade it in the future as hyper-competition[23] accelerates.

1.2 Aim and Approach

Our aim in this book is to build a theoretical and practical understanding of how re-internationalized firms identify and pursue international growth opportunities by innovating and re-configuring their business models (BMs) in the aftermath of their de-internationalization. We develop inductively an interdisciplinary framework (Fig. 1.2) to offer IB and BMI researchers a path to advance a holistic understanding of the relationship

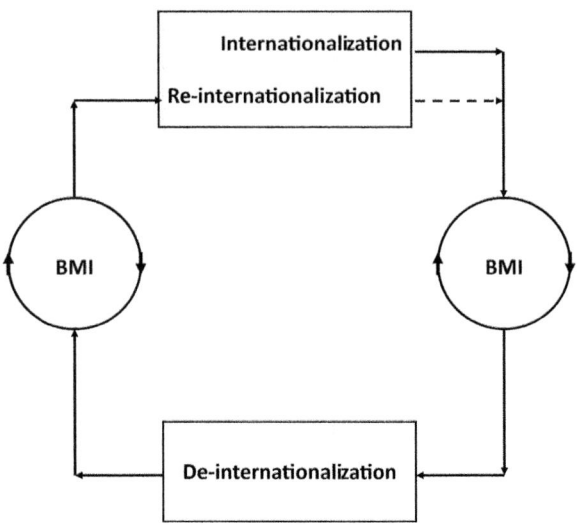

Fig. 1.1 A relationship between cross-border activity and BMI

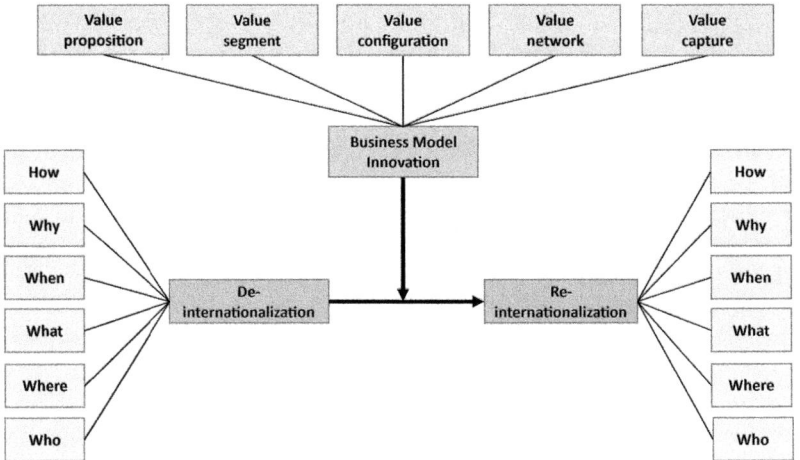

Fig. 1.2 De-internationalization, re-internationalization, and BMI intersection framework

between de-internationalization and re-internationalization through BMI theoretical lenses. We ground inductively our interdisciplinary framework in the extant empirical and theoretical knowledge derived from IB and BMI disciplines. The framework explains how firms building on their de-internationalization experience can reconfigure their BMs to pursue re-internationalization, eventually aiming to further their international growth. The framework maps the key drivers of de-internationalization and re-internationalization, namely, *why, how, what, where, when*, and *who*, and the BMI five value drivers, namely, *value proposition, value segment, value configuration, value network*, and *value capture*.

To understand the *why*, decision-makers delve into external and internal reasons that inform their de-internationalization and re-internatio nalization decisions.[24] Considering the *how*, decision-makers assess whether to de-internationalize or re-internationalize completely or partially through de-investing, de-exporting, indirect, trade-in value-added, exporting, or mode change combinations.[25] The *when* is about the demand from decision-makers to assess the timing of commitment to de-internationalize or re-internationalize, mitigate the errors of commission and omission,[26] and assess the real point of no return and false point of no return.[27] Considering the *what*, decision-makers decide what parts of their firms' value chain ought to be de-internationalized and eventually re-internationalized.[28] The *where* addresses the location of de-internatio nalization and re-internationalization; for example, decision-makers assess whether to backshore, nearshore, or reshore.[29] Understanding the *who* is about understanding decision-makers at the headquarters or subsidiary levels, and their rationale to commit to and act on de-internationalization and re-internationalization or failure to commit and act, escalating their commitments to a failing course of de-internationalization or re-internationalization.[30]

Understanding how firms building on their de-internationalization experience can innovate and reconfigure their business models to pursue re-internationalization is vital to the firms' survival and further international growth. At the same time, by borrowing from BMI to understand de-internationalization and re-internationalization, we contribute back to BMI research domain that is in need for new models and testable propositions[31] which have scarcely been explored in the IB context, e.g., how retailers rebuild their business logic in new host countries.[32] We also contribute to BM literature an understanding of how firms may innovate and renew their existing and future cross-border postures by designing new or reconfiguring existing business models.[33] Within this mutual cross-fertilization, we call on IB and BM researchers to set and actively engage in a research program to study this complex, but promising, intersection between de-internationalization, re-internationalization, and BMI.

1.3 Book Structure

The next chapter, "*Internationalization*," introduces internationalization to set the stage for understanding its relation to de-internationalization and re-internationalization. We define internationalization as "*a process and a state that allow firms to gradually or instantly cross national borders to commit to diverse relationships with key stakeholders in international contexts.*" We "unpack" this definition and offer a fine-grained discussion of its key concepts: process and state; gradual or instant; crossing national borders; commitment and context. We start connecting some of these concepts (e.g., escalation of commitment, dominant logic, and organizational gestalt) to de-internationalization and re-internationalization for the purpose of exemplifying the holistic view of firm cross-border activity we adopt in this book.

"*De-internationalization*," which is the focus of the next chapter, is routinely perceived as a failure, an undesired enterprise, by many—entrepreneurs, CEOs, investors, and policy makers. We depart from this view and argue that as part of the cross-border activity of the firm, de-internationalization can contribute to the overall growth of the firm. For this view to get "traction," it is pivotal for key stakeholders to acknowledge, embrace, and encourage de-internationalization rather than ignore and/or avoid it. In this chapter, we define de-internationalization as "*the firm's capacity to reconfigure its organizational gestalt*[34] *before or at the real point of no return.*"[35] We build on the two errors of de-internationalization: *an error of commission* (De-e1), which is when a firm should not have de-internationalized earlier but did so, and *an error of omission* (De-e2), which is when a firm should have de-internationalized earlier but failed to do so.[36] We further define and discuss the de-internationalization process, its types, "hows," and "whys." The frameworks we present in this chapter, e.g., de-internationalization typology, modes, and drivers, become the foundations for understanding the intersection of re-internationalization, IB, and BMI in the following chapters.

In the next chapter, we turn to "*Re-internationalization*," the third type of cross-border activity of the firm. Compared to internationalization and de-internationalization, re-internationalization is less understood and researched and has yet to be studied systematically. To start filling in this gap and contribute to our exploration of the IB-BM/BMI intersection, we offer a definition and a typology of re-internationalization. We define re-internationalization as "*a process and a state that allow a firm to re-configure its pattern, capacity, and logic to gradually or instantly cross national borders following total or partial de-internationalization.*" Building on de-internationalization error correcting mechanisms (De-e1 and De-e2), we define re-internationalization correcting mechanisms: an *error of commission* (Re-e1), when a firm commits too early to re-internationalization, and an *error of omission* (Re-e2), when a firm fails to take (full) advantage of a new IB market opportunity. We develop a typology founded on a conjecture that re-internationalization depends on the success and/or failure of internationalization and de-internationalization. We cross-tabulated these two dimensions and their properties to arrive at re-internationalization typology and its four types: *imitating, balancing, rejuvenating*, and *taking time-off*.

The "*Business Model Innovation*" chapter introduces BMI to the reader. It defines BMI, its types, and configuration drivers. We define BMI as "*a process of reconfiguring organizational gestalt*" and introduce BMI strategies: abstracting, zooming-in, zooming-out, and iterating. To explore the intersection of de-internationalization and re-internationalization (which is the focus of the next two chapters), we employ *BMI types*:[37] *(semi) closed BMI*; *open BMI*; *from scratch BMI*; and *network level BMI*. We employ the BMI *configurations framework*[38] that categorizes BM configurations into Five Value Drivers: value proposition; value segment; value configuration; value network; and value capture.[39] BM configurations help decision-makers learn from proven "formulae" that were tried and tested by other firms across industries and markets, as well as how to adapt and adopt them to escape entrapment and "open the blinds" to innovate their firms' BMs.

In the next two chapters, "*BMI and De-internationalization*" and "*BMI and Re-internationalization*," we bring de-internationalization, re-internationalization, and BMI together. In the "*BMI and De-internationalization*" chapter, we employ the 5-V framework to understand the "hows" and the "whys" of de-internationalization within the scope of de-internationalization types: total and partial withdrawal from international markets. In this process, we highlight various de-internationalization strategies and respective BM value drivers that are affected by intended de-internationalization, e.g., to optimize exit modes, foreign markets, operations, or fundamentally redesign the BM.

In the *"BMI and Re-internationalization,"* chapter, we continue employing the 5-V framework to understand the re-internationalization-BMI intersection by linking value proposition, value segment, value configuration, value network, and value capture drivers to re-internationalization. The main argument is that understanding, for example, the "whys" of de-internationalization through BM value drivers can inform the BM configurations of re-internationalization, such as the "hows" of re-internationalization, shaping its patterns, and capacities. We make the first attempt toward the development of the IB-BMI framework by conceptualizing the relation between the "hows" of re-internationalization and the "whys" of re-internationalization through a moderation effect of BMI value drivers and configuration types.

In the concluding chapter, *"Toward an IB-BM Research Program,"* we first offer concluding remarks, highlighting key substantive contributions we made to IB core areas, internationalization, de-internationalization, and re-internationalization, and to the IB-BM intersection, namely, de-internationalization, re-internationalization, and BMI intersection. We then put forward a proposal for an IB-BM research program to bring together academics, practitioners, and policy makers to study holistically the relation between internationalization, de-internationalization, re-internationalization, and BMI in a VUCA world. We develop a conceptual framework of the program and exemplify its adoption by cross-tabulating internationalization gestalt and value drivers to define a set of research questions that can be pursued in the program. Such an embryonic research program will create more questions than answers, making it an interesting avenue for future inter-disciplinary research and practice pondering.

Notes

1. Bauman (2007)
2. Bauman (2007, p. 1).
3. The Economist (2021).
4. Petersen and Welch (2003), Welch and Luostarinen (1988).
5. Gaur et al. (2019), Welch and Welch (2009), Yang et al. (2015).
6. Kumar (2020), Kumar and Srivastava (2020).
7. Bernini et al. (2016), Berry (2013), Dachs et al. (2019); Konara and Ganotakis (2020); Mohr et al. (2018), Tang et al. (2021).

8. For example, Bernini et al. (2016), Chen et al. (2019), Javalgi et al. (2011), Surdu et al. (2019), Welch and Welch (2009).
9. Berry (2013), Mohr et al. (2018), Soule et al. (2014), Turcan (2013), Vissak (2010).
10. Benito and Welch (1997), Bernini et al. (2016), Turcan (2013).
11. Dachs and Zanker (2014), Vissak (2010).
12. Benito and Welch (1997), Calof and Beamish (1995), Welch and Luostarinen (1988).
13. Benito and Welch (1997).
14. Turcan (2013).
15. Turcan, Fast, Lowe and Dholakia (2024).
16. Turcan (2006).
17. Kafouros et al. (2022), Turcan (2006).
18. Turcan (2003, 2006).
19. Johansson (2017), Wilson (1998).
20. Adapted from Turcan (2003).
21. Osterwalder and Pigneur (2010).
22. Cao et al. (2018), Kumar and Srivastava (2020).
23. D'Aveni (1994).
24. Shaver and Flyer (2000), Tang et al. (2021).
25. Benito and Welch (1997), Schmid and Morschett (2020).
26. Casson (1986).
27. Turcan (2013).
28. Li and Liu (2015).
29. Lampon et al. (2017), Valentino et al. (2019).
30. Steensma and Lyles (2000).
31. Leonidou et al. (2018).
32. Cao et al. (2018).
33. Massa and Tucci (2013), Osiyevskyy and Dewald (2015).
34. Organizational gestalt is defined by pattern, capacity, and logic of the firm. Each cross-border activity type, that is, , internationalization, de-internationalization, and re-internationalization, has its own gestalt.
35. Turcan (2006).
36. Casson (1986).
37. Taran et al. (2022).
38. Taran et al. (2016).
39. Based on Taran et al. (2016, 2022).

References

Bauman, Z. (2007). *Liquid times: Living in an age of uncertainty*. Polity Press.
Benito, G., & Welch, L. (1997). De-internationalization. *Management International Review, 37*, 7–25.

Bernini, M., Du, J., & Love, J. H. (2016). Explaining intermittent exporting: Exit and conditional re-entry in export markets. *Journal of International Business Studies, 47*(9), 1058–1076.

Berry, H. (2013). When do firms divest foreign operations? *Organization Science, 24*(1), 246–261.

Calof, J. L., & Beamish, P. W. (1995). Adapting to foreign markets: Explaining internationalization. *International Business Review, 4*(2), 115–131.

Cao, L., Navare, J., & Jin, Z. (2018). Business model innovation: How the international retailers rebuild their core business logic in a new host country. *International Business Review, 27*(3), 543–562.

Casson, M. (1986). International divestment and restructuring decisions: With special reference to the motor industry. *International Labour Organization*. Working Paper 40.

Chen, J., Sousa, C. M., & He, X. (2019). Export market re-entry: Time-out period and price/quality dynamisms. *Journal of World Business, 54*(2), 154–168.

D'Aveni, R. A. (1994). *Hypercompetition*. The Free Press.

Dachs, B., Kinkel, S., & Jäger, A. (2019). Bringing it all back home? Backshoring of manufacturing activities and the adoption of Industry 4.0 technologies. *Journal of World Business, 54*(6), 1–15.

Dachs, B., & Zanker, C. (2014). Backshoring of production activities in European manufacturing. *European Manufacturing Survey*. Retrieved May 2021, from https://t.ly/jDaqN

Gaur, A. S., Pattnaik, C., Singh, D., & Lee, J. Y. (2019). Internalization advantage and subsidiary performance: The role of business group affiliation and host country characteristics. *Journal of International Business Studies, 50*(8), 1253–1282.

Javalgi, R. G., Deligonul, S., Dixit, A., & Cavusgil, S. T. (2011). International market reentry: A review and research framework. *International Business Review, 20*(4), 377–393.

Johansson, F. (2017). *The Medici effect, with a new preface and discussion guide: What elephants and epidemics can teach us about innovation*. Harvard Business Review Press.

Kafouros, M., Cavusgil, S. T., Devinney, T. M., Ganotakis, P., & Fainshmidt, S. (2022). Cycles of de-internationalization and re-internationalization: Towards an integrative framework. *Journal of World Business, 57*(1), 101257.

Konara, P., & Ganotakis, P. (2020). Firm-specific resources and foreign divestments via sell-offs: Value is in the eye of the beholder. *Journal of Business Research, 110*, 423–434.

Kumar, V. (2020). Global implications of cause-related loyalty marketing. *International Marketing Review, 37*(4), 747–772.

Kumar, V., & Srivastava, R. (2020). New perspectives on business model innovations in emerging markets. *Journal of the Academy of Marketing Science, 48*, 815–825.

Lampon, J. F., Cabanelas, P., & Carballo-Cruz, F. (2017). A model for international production relocation: Multinationals' operational flexibility and requirements at production plant level. *Journal of Business Research, 77*, 95–101.

Leonidou, L. C., Katsikeas, C. S., Samiee, S., & Aykol, B. (2018). International marketing research: A state-of-the-art review and the way forward. *Advances in Global Marketing*, 3–33.

Li, R., & Liu, Z. (2015). What causes the divestment of multinational companies in China? A subsidiary perspective. *Journal of Business Theory and Practice, 3*(1), 81–89.

Massa, L., & Tucci, C. L. (2013). Business model innovation. In M. Dodgson, D. M. Gann, & N. Phillips (Eds.), *The Oxford handbook of innovation management* (pp. 420–441). Oxford University Press.

Mohr, A., Batsakis, G., & Stone, Z. (2018). Explaining the effect of rapid internationalization on horizontal foreign divestment in the retail sector: An extended Penrosean perspective.

Osiyevskyy, O., & Dewald, J. (2015). Explorative versus exploitative business model change: The cognitive antecedents of firm level responses to disruptive innovation. *Strategic Entrepreneurship Journal, 9*, 58–78.

Osterwalder, A., & Pigneur, Y. (2010). *Business model generation: A handbook for visionaries, game changers, and challengers*. John Wiley and Sons.

Petersen, B., & Welch, L. S. (2003). International business development and the internet, post-hype. *Management International Review, 43*(1), 7–29.

Schmid, D., & Morschett, D. (2020). Decades of research on foreign subsidiary divestment: What do we really know about its antecedents? *International Business Review, 29*(4), 101653.

Shaver, J. M., & Flyer, F. (2000). Agglomeration economies, firm heterogeneity, and foreign direct investment in the United States. *Strategic Management Journal, 21*(12), 1175–1193.

Soule, S. A., Swaminathan, A., & Tihanyi, L. (2014). The diffusion of foreign divestment from Burma. *Strategic Management Journal, 35*(7), 1032–1052.

Steensma, H. K., & Lyles, M. A. (2000). Explaining IJV survival in a transitional economy through social exchange and knowledge-based perspectives. *Strategic Management Journal, 21*(8), 831–851.

Surdu, I., Mellahi, K., & Glaister, K. W. (2019). Once bitten, not necessarily shy? Determinants of foreign market re-entry commitment strategies. *Journal of International Business Studies, 50*(3), 393–422.

Tang, R. W., Zhu, Y., Cai, H., & Han, J. (2021). De-internationalization: A thematic review and the directions forward. *Management International Review, 61*(3), 267–312.

Taran, Y., Boer, H., & Nielsen, C. (2022). *The business model innovation process: Preparation, organization and management*. Routledge.

Taran, Y., Nielsen, C., Montemari, M., Thomsen, P., & Paolone, F. (2016). Business model configurations: A five-V framework to map out potential innovation routes. *European Journal of Innovation Management, 19*(4), 492–527.

The Economist. (2021, December 18). The new normal is already here. Get used to it. *The Economist, 441*(9276), 13.

Turcan, R., Fast, M., Lowe, A., & Dholakia, N. (2024). *The art of theory building: Knowledge creation in management research.* Palgrave Macmillan.

Turcan, R. V. (2003). De-internationalization and the small firm. In C. Wheeler, F. McDonald, & I. Greaves (Eds.), *Internationalization: Firms strategies and management* (pp. 208–222). Palgrave.

Turcan, R. V. (2006). De-internationalization of small high-technology firms: An international entrepreneurship perspective. Doctoral dissertation, University of Strathclyde, Glasgow, UK.

Turcan, R. V. (2013). The philosophy of turning points: A case of de-internationalization. *Advances in International Management, 26*, 219–235.

Valentino, A., Schmitt, J., Koch, B., & Nell, P. C. (2019). Leaving home: An institutional perspective on intermediary HQ relocations. *Journal of World Business, 54*(4), 273–284.

Vissak, T. (2010). Nonlinear internationalization: A neglected topic in international business research. In *The past, present and future of international business and management.* Emerald Group Publishing.

Welch, C. L., & Welch, L. S. (2009). Re-internationalization: Exploration and conceptualisation. *International Business Review, 18*(6), 567–577.

Welch, L. S., & Luostarinen, R. (1988). Internationalization: Evolution of a concept. *Journal of General Management, 14*(2), 34–55.

Wilson, E. O. (1998). *Consilience: The unity of knowledge.* Knopf.

Yang, J. Y., Li, J., & Delios, A. (2015). Will a second mouse get the cheese? Learning from early entrants' failures in a foreign market. *Organization Science, 26*(3), 908–922.

CHAPTER 2

Internationalization

The sea has such extraordinary moods that sometimes you feel this is the only sort of life—and 10 minutes later you're praying for death.
—Prince Philip

2.1 Setting the Compass for an Unknown Adventure

Internationalization appeals to many and for various reasons: entrepreneurs to legitimate their new ventures; CEOs to boost their firms' growth; and policy makers to stimulate economic growth. It is a mature phenomenon with well-established theories and theoretical frameworks[1] that can predict and explain the internationalization behavior of firms. Together with de-internationalization and re-internationalization, it is part of a firm's cross-border activity[2] that falls within the scope of IB. Internationalization, de-internationalization, and re-internationalization are distinct types of cross-border activities (Fig. 1.1), and so are the antecedents, motives, and modes of these cross-border activity types.[3] In this book, we adopt this view and apply it to analyze how business model configurations can help enhance the understanding of the relationship between de-internationalization and re-internationalization. Internationalization *as a process and a state allows firms to gradually or instantly cross national borders to* commit to diverse relationships with key stakeholders in international contexts. This "heavily loaded" definition of internationalization needs "unpacking."

2.2 Process and State

The *duality* of internationalization as a *process* and a *state* can be explained by the two dimensions of internationalization of the firm: *internationalization pattern* and *internationalization capacity*.[4] The former is concerned with *how, why, when, what, where,* and *who* of internationalization and includes, inter alia, foreign market entry modes such as exporting, franchising, strategic alliances, joint ventures, acquisitions, greenfield, and brownfield investments[5] or a combination of modes;[6] product and/or service mix of the value delivered internationally; and timing and pace of internationalization. The latter refers to a configuration, inter alia, of resource and capability (e.g., technological, human, and financial) of the firm, its processes and structures, internationalization strategy, experience, and motivation of its key decision-makers in conducting international business.

2.3 Gradual Or Instant

A gradual approach to internationalization implies a measured design, setup, and pursuit of an internationalization capacity and pattern configuration. Firms pursuing gradual internationalization focus on gradual acquisition, integration, and exploitation of conceptual and experiential knowledge, tangible and intangible resources, and dynamic and substantive capabilities related to a foreign market entry or multiple foreign market entries. Their experiential learning is gradual. Through such gradual experiential learning, firms seek to minimize the "psychic distance" between home and target, foreign market contexts. This process implies identifying factors that "prevent ... or disturb ... firms learning about and understanding a foreign environment,"[7] grasping and mitigating their impact on a firm's internationalization posture. Consequently, these firms would gradually enter foreign markets, starting with those that are "psychically" close and postpone entering "psychically" distant ones.[8] Concurrently, they may adopt a sequential approach to entry modes, starting with those that require less commitment (e.g., exporting and licensing) and are less risky and then gradually moving to entry modes that demand greater commitment (e.g., joint ventures and acquisitions) and entail higher risk (Vignette 2.1).

> **Vignette 2.1 Nike—Diversified market entry modes strategy**
> Nike is a multinational firm headquartered near Beaverton, Oregon, in the athletic footwear and apparel business.[9] It is one of the world's largest suppliers in this category and a major manufacturer of sports equipment. Over the years, Nike has experimented with various foreign market entry modes.
>
> In the 1960s, Nike followed an exporting strategy to European and Asian regions. This lower-commitment mode aimed to "test the waters" in these markets. Through the 1960s and, increasingly, during the 1970s–1980s, it steadily increased its commitments in foreign markets by focusing on international expansion through contract manufacturing in South Korea and Taiwan[10] to scale up its core footwear and apparel offerings and sales.
>
> During the 1980s–1990s, Nike steadily increased its international commitment by forming joint ventures with local partners and firms. Examples include joint ventures with firms in South Korea, China, and Brazil. To further expand its global market presence, distribution networks, and offerings, Nike initiated various acquisition strategies, many of which were of American brands with global reach (e.g., Cole Haan in 1988;[11] Bauer Hockey in 1994);[12] Umbro acquisition, a UK-headquarters-based acquisition, though, came much later in 2007. Since 1990s, Nike has continued to invest internationally, relying heavily on contract manufacturers in various countries around the globe.[13]

There are firms such as international new ventures and born globals that internationalize instantly, right or immediately after their inception[14] or the inception of a new international venture idea.[15] Psychic distance is not a factor that can limit the timing and speed of these firms' internationalization. Their internationalization capacity and pattern configurations can be designed and set up to enter "psychically distant" international markets and commit to high risk, high cost, and high control entry modes very early in their life, usually within three years from their start up.[16] These international new firms and their internationalization posture co-emerge at a "high speed." So does their absorptive capacity, the ability to recognize the value of new knowledge and assimilate and apply it.[17] These are examples of strategic experimentation[18] that such international new firms pursue to build an organizational gestalt[19] or a dominant logic[20] for the first time. Instant internationalization may occur in "grown-up" or "old" firms, well established in their home markets. As a result of a critical event,[21] a well-established, domestic firm would internationalize quickly at or immediately after the inception of a new international business idea.[22] These firms are "born-again" globals.[23] There is a third type of international new firms—born-global again.[24] These are firms that re-internationalize at, during, or immediately after their de-internationalization (Vignette 2.2).

Vignette 2.2 Jolla—Re-born global

Jolla, a tech firm from Finland, focuses on innovative operating system (OS) solutions and "AppSupport," which allows Android apps to run on any Linux platform.[25] It was formed in 2011. Building on Nokia's heritage, especially in the MeeGo OS,[26] a group of former Nokia employees had a shared vision to create a new mobile device based on a new OS. Jolla was conceived as an alternative or a competition to the dominant Android and iOS. Two years after its inception, in November 2013, it introduced the "Jolla smartphone" (manufactured in China) that ran on its own proprietary Sailfish OS. The Jolla smartphone entered 36 markets during its first year.[27]

Although the new offering attracted significant international excitement, the first born global "sailing" attempt didn't get traction. The target markets, including its primary market, the EU, and their ecosystems were dominated by giants such as Samsung and Apple. It was difficult for newcomers to succeed due to the liabilities of foreignness, newness, and smallness[28] that Jolla faced in these markets, hindering its capacity to compete effectively; project delays didn't help either.[29]

Barely staying afloat, in 2015, Jolla chose to scale back its operations[30] and pivoted its business model from mobile phones and OS to OS only, offering its Sailfish OS software solutions as a licensing model.[31]

Continuously "braving the waves," Jolla followed an exclusive mobile OS licensing model for local market implementations[32] and managed a comeback by transforming itself into a pure software solution provider. Their continuously improved Sailfish OS found new life in, for example, Sony Xperia X in 2017, and later expanded to support variants of the Xperia XA2, Xperia 10 devices, Gemini PDA, and others.[33] Jolla's re-born global journey continues, expanding its offerings, international market scope, and partnerships.

2.4 Crossing National Borders

When a firm crosses its national border for the first time, it undertakes its *first-time* internationalization. Crossing national borders beyond that point is a *continual* internationalization of the firm. *Crossing national borders* is one of the many development or growth strategies firms may adopt. A set of such strategies consists of stability, expansion, retrenchment, and combinations of these three.[34] A firm pursuing a stability development strategy seeks to remain in the same business with a similar level of effort, pursuing existing objectives and incremental improvement of performance. Expansion development strategy is about growth into new business areas and/or new markets, aiming to increase sales, profits, or market share at a higher rate than those of competitors. In pursuit of a retrenchment development strategy, a firm will withdraw from some or all of its business components, aiming to create a smaller organization, a leaner management structure, and more efficient production and marketing. A firm may pursue a combination of these three development strategies simultaneously or sequentially (Vignette 2.3).

> **Vignette 2.3 Procter & Gamble—Dual growth strategy of retrenchment and expansion**
>
> Procter & Gamble (P&G) is a multinational consumer goods firm, founded in 1837.[35] From inception, it grew solely within its domestic, US market.
>
> At the beginning of the twentieth century, P&G started to diversify its offerings portfolio. In 1915, P&G opened its first production site outside of the United States, in Canada, and in 1930, it bought Thomas Hedley & Company, an English Soap firm.[36]
>
> The acquisition of Gillette in 2005 boosted its international expansion and global presence.[37] In 2018, P&G acquired the Consumer Health Business of Merck KGaA, located in Darmstadt, Germany, for approximately €3.4 billion.[38]
>
> Having recognized the need for strategic adaptation, P&G followed a combined approach as part of its cross-border strategy, e.g., expanding core brands and retrenching other brands. In its 2017 annual report, P&G informed its shareholders that it had completed "streamlining and strengthening … [its] product portfolio. In just over two years, [it] divested, discontinued or consolidated 105 brands, and built market capitalization as [it] executed this significant restructure."[39] This led to a consolidated portfolio of 65 key brands in 10 business categories.

2.5 Commitment

Commitment is one of the key dimensions of a firm's internationalization, specifically, and cross-border activity, in general.[40] It is also a double-edged sword, as it can both facilitate and inhibit internationalization. A commitment to design and pursue a certain configuration of internationalization pattern and capacity implies, for example, deciding on which foreign market or markets to enter, the timing and pacing of foreign market entry, and the degree or extent of risk and control of the entry modes and/or entry mode combinations needed to enter a foreign market. A commitment to a first-time internationalization substantially differs from a commitment to ongoing internationalization. In the latter, the commitment to scope, costs, and risks encompasses a diverse mix of configurations of patterns, capacities, and logics, as well as maintenance of existing and/or development of new ones.

A commitment to non-equity modes of entry differs perceptibly from a commitment to equity-modes of entry, such as joint-ventures or wholly owned subsidiaries. The latter are riskier, offer a higher level of control over the cross-border activity, and usually are pursued when firms can acquire, integrate, and exploit conceptual and experiential knowledge related to cross-border activities. A pursuit of an entry mode might give a "prima facie" indication of the firm's commitment. However, this might be misleading, as firms may, and most likely will, engage in the pursuit of a combination or a package of entry modes.[41]

At the same time, the continued commitment of firms to their internationalization patterns and capacities poses a conundrum. The probability of de-internationalization declines as the firm's commitment to its foreign operations increases.[42] A firm's continued commitment is dependent on dominant logic, a way in which decision-makers conceptualize their businesses and make critical resource allocation decisions.[43] Once established and pursued, a firm's commitment to context-tailored organizational gestalt and dominant logic can act as a trap,[44] a blinder,[45] or an entrapment,[46] preventing the firm from changing or unlearning its international organizational gestalt and dominant logic and eventually de-internationalize and successfully re-internationalize.[47] This relationship comes to the fore, especially when we consider the inverse relationship between (1) de-internationalization and internationalization[48] and (2) agility and entrapment.[49]

2.6 Context

To understand the context within which firms internationalize, de-internationalize, and, eventually, re-internationalize, it is pivotal to clarify what we mean by "context." We define context as "situational opportunities and constraints that affect the occurrence and meaning of organizational behavior as well as functional relationships between variables."[50] Host country institutions, legal, normative, and cognitive,[51] can offer and/or create opportunities to attract foreign firms and, at the same time, may sanction behaviors that do not comply with and/or follow the rules of the game. Within the scope of this definition, we view internationalization, de-internationalization, and re-internationalization as dependent on a firm's context-tailored organizational gestalt consisting of mutually supportive organizational system elements combined with appropriate resources and behavioral patterns[52] (cross-border capacity and pattern respectively).

2.7 Concluding Remarks

Internationalization is a type of cross-border activity of a firm. In this chapter, we defined it and "unpacked" its key concepts: process and state; gradual or instant; crossing national borders; commitment and context. The way these concepts are configured and implemented impacts the international and overall performance of a firm, its ability to sustain that performance, and reconfigure its organizational gestalt—pattern, capacity and logic—including in the face of an international market withdrawal. We introduced two types of internationalization: first-time and continual internationalization. This conceptualization is based on a conjecture that there is a substantial difference between an internationalization gestalt configured and pursued for the first time by a firm, and an internationalization gestalt re-configured and pursued by a firm following its first-time internationalization. From this, we further conjecture that de-internatio nalization and re-internationalization of a firm will be also significantly different following first-time or continual internationalization. The former might be less "dramatic" and "painful." Understanding these two types of internationalization and their respective organizational gestalts will help researchers and practitioners better understand, inter alia, de-internationalization and re-internationalization of the firm.

NOTES

1. Bell et al. (2003), Benito and Welch (1997), Buckley and Casson (1976, 2009), Casson (1986, 1990), Cavusgil (1980), Dunning (1977, 2000), Hennart (1985, 2012), Johanson and Wiedersheim-Paul (1975), Johanson and Vahlne (1977, 1990, 2009), Johanson and Mattsson (1988, 1992), Jones (1999), Jones and Coviello (2005), Madsen and Servais (1997), McDougall et al. (1994), McDougall and Oviatt (2000), Turcan (2006), Vahlne and Johanson (2020), Welch and Luostarinen (1993).
2. This view can also be found in Boddewyn (1985), Calof and Beamish (1995), Turcan (2003, 2006), Welch and Luostarinen (1988).
3. Turcan (2003, 2006).
4. Petersen and Welch (2003), Welch and Luostarinen (1988).
5. Root (1994).
6. Benito et al. (2009).
7. Nordström and Vahlne (1992), p. 3).
8. Brewer (2007), Johanson and Vahlne (1977, 1990, 2009), O'Grady and Lane (1996).
9. Nike (2024).
10. Ascoly and Zeldenrust (2003).
11. Adelson (1988).
12. Austen (2008).
13. Nike (2024).
14. Jones et al. (2011).
15. Turcan (2006).
16. Turcan (2013).
17. Cohen and Levinthal (1990).
18. Nicholls-Nixon et al. (2000).
19. Covin and Slevin (1997).
20. Bettis and Prahalad (1995).
21. An event can be considered critical if it deviates significantly, either positively or negatively, from what is normal or expected (Edvardsson, 1992).
22. Turcan (2006).
23. Bell et al. (2003).
24. Turcan (2006).
25. Jolla (2024).
26. Sailfish (2024).
27. Sailfish (2024).
28. Choi et al. (2021) and Gimenez-Fernandez et al. (2020).
29. Saarnio (2016).
30. Techcrunch (2015).
31. Sailfish (2024).

32. Sailfish (2024).
33. Jolla Devices (2024).
34. Young et al. (1989).
35. Forbes (2024).
36. Horowitz (2011).
37. Butler (2020).
38. SEC (2018).
39. Procter and Gamble (2017).
40. Turcan (2003, 2006).
41. Benito et al. (2009).
42. Benito and Welch (1997), Turcan (2006).
43. Bettis and Prahalad (1995).
44. Chesbrough (2003).
45. Prahalad (2004).
46. Drummond (2004), Turcan (2013).
47. Escalation situations include repeated decision-making in the face of negative feedback about prior resource allocations, uncertainty surrounding the likelihood of goal attainment, and choice about whether to continue (Brockner, 1992). Escalating commitment has been attributed to four sets of forces that come into play over time: (1) project, e.g., closing costs and salvage value of a cross-border activity; (2) psychological, e.g., reinforcement traps, information biasing, and self-justification; (3) social, e.g., cultural and/or organizational norms and job security; and (4) organizational, e.g., degree and level of support and embeddedness of a cross-border activity in the firm (Drummond, 1994; Ross & Staw, 1993).
48. Benito and Welch (1997).
49. Turcan (2013).
50. Johns (2006, p. 386).
51. Scott (2013).
52. Covin and Slevin (1997).

References

Adelson, R. (1988, April 26). Company news: Cole to Nike for $80 million. *The New York Times*. https://t.ly/RyYDs

Ascoly, N., & Zeldenrust, I. (2003). East and Southeast Asia regional labor research report. Retrieved February 28, 2024, from https://t.ly/q81oY

Austen, I. (2008, February 28). Hockey fan and investor buys Bauer from Nike. *The New York Times*. https://t.ly/fFibE

Bell, J., McNaughton, R., Young, S., & Crick, D. (2003). Towards an integrative model of small firm internationalisation. *Journal of International Entrepreneurship, 1*(4), 339–362.

Benito, G., & Welch, L. (1997). De-internationalization. *Management International Review, 37*, 7–25.

Benito, G. R., Petersen, B., & Welch, L. S. (2009). Towards more realistic conceptualisations of foreign operation modes. *Journal of International Business Studies, 40*, 1455–1470.

Bettis, R. A., & Prahalad, C. K. (1995). The dominant logic: Retrospective and extension. *Strategic Management Journal, 16*(1), 5–14.

Boddewyn, J. (1985). Theories of foreign direct investment and divestment: A classificatory note. *Management International Review, 25*(1), 57–65.

Brewer, P. A. (2007). Operationalizing psychic distance: A revised approach. *Journal of International Marketing, 15*(1), 44–66.

Brockner, J. (1992). The escalation of commitment to a failing course of action: Toward theoretical progress. *Academy of Management Review, 17*(1), 39–62.

Buckley, P. J., & Casson, M. (1976). *The future of the multinational enterprise*. Macmillan.

Buckley, P. J., & Casson, M. (2009). The internalisation theory of the multinational enterprise: A review of the progress of a research agenda after 30 years. *Journal of International Business Studies, 40*(9), 1563–1580.

Butler, D. (2020). History of Procter & Gamble: Timeline and facts. *The Street*. https://t.ly/NpOYG

Calof, J. L., & Beamish, P. W. (1995). Adapting to foreign markets: Explaining internationalization. *International Business Review, 4*(2), 115–131.

Casson, M. (1986). International divestment and restructuring decisions: With special reference to the motor industry. *International Labour Organization*. Working Paper 40.

Casson, M. (1990). *Enterprise and competitiveness: A system view of international business*. Clarendon.

Cavusgil, S. (1980). On the internationalization process of firms. *European Research, 8*(6), 273–281.

Chesbrough, H. (2003). *Open innovation: The new imperative for creating and profiting from technology*. Harvard Business School Press.

Choi, H., Lee, E., & Park, Y. R. (2021). Determinants of the internationalization of born-digital firms. *Korean Social Science Journal, 48*(3), 97–117.

Cohen, W. M., & Levinthal, D. A. (1990). Absorptive capacity: A new perspective on learning and innovation. *Administrative Science Quarterly, 35*(1), 128–152.

Covin, J., & Slevin, D. (1997). High growth transitions: Theoretical perspectives and suggested directions. In D. Sexton & R. Smilor (Eds.), *Entrepreneurship 2000* (pp. 99–126). Upstart Publishing.

Drummond, H. (1994). Too little too late: A case study of escalation in decision making. *Organization Studies, 15*(4), 591–607.

Drummond, H. (2004). See you next week? A study of entrapment in a small business. *International Small Business Journal, 22*(5), 487–502.

Dunning, J. (2000). The eclectic paradigm as an envelope for economic and business theories of MNE activity. *International Business Review, 9*(1), 163–190.

Dunning, J. H. (1977). Trade, location of economic activity and the MNE: A search for an eclectic approach. In B. Ohlin, P.-O. Hesselborn, & P. M. Wijkman (Eds.), *The international allocation of economic activity* (pp. 395–418). Holmes and Meier.

Edvardsson, B. (1992). Service breakdowns: A study of critical incidents in an airline. *International Journal of Service Industry Management, 3*(4), 17–29.

Forbes. (2024). Procter & Gamble. Retrieved March 4, 2024, from https://t.ly/_riPD

Gimenez-Fernandez, E. M., Sandulli, F. D., & Bogers, M. (2020). Unpacking liabilities of newness and smallness in innovative start-ups: Investigating the differences in innovation performance between new and older small firms. *Research Policy, 49*(10), 104049.

Hennart, J.-F. (1985). *The theory of multinational enterprise* (2nd ed.). University of Michigan Press.

Hennart, J.-F. (2012). Emerging market multinationals and the theory of the multinational enterprise. *Global Strategy Journal, 2*(3), 168–187.

Horowitz, A. (2011, February 15). How Procter & Gamble became the maker of everything you buy for your house. *Business Insider*. Retrieved March 4, 2024, from https://t.ly/8_4eY

Johanson, J., & Mattsson, L. G. (1988). Internationalization in industrial systems: A network approach. In N. Hood & J.-E. Vahlne (Eds.), *Strategies in global competition* (pp. 287–314). Croom Helm.

Johanson, J., & Mattsson, L.-G. (1992). Network positions and strategic action: An analytical framework. In B. Axelsson & G. Easton (Eds.), *Industrial networks: A new view of reality* (pp. 205–217). Routledge.

Johanson, J., & Vahlne, J.-E. (1977). The internationalization process of the firm: A model of knowledge development and increasing foreign market commitments. *Journal of International Business Studies, 8*(1), 23–32.

Johanson, J., & Vahlne, J.-E. (1990). The mechanism of internationalization. *International Marketing Review, 7*(4), 11–24.

Johanson, J., & Vahlne, J.-E. (2009). The Uppsala internationalization process model revisited: From liability of foreignness to liability of outsidership. *Journal of International Business Studies, 40*(9).

Johanson, J., & Wiedersheim-Paul, F. (1975, October). The internationalization of the firm: Four Swedish cases. *Journal of Management Studies*, 305–322.

Johns, G. (2006). The essential impact of context on organizational behavior. *The Academy of Management Review, 31*(2), 386–408.

Jolla Devices. (2024). Here are the official Sailfish devices, the one maintained and updated by Jolla. Retrieved March 20, 2024, https://t.ly/SXzxb

Jones, M. (1999). The internationalization of small high-technology firms. *Journal of International Marketing, 7*(4), 15–41.

Jones, M. V., Coviello, N., & Tang, Y. K. (2011). International entrepreneurship research (1989–2009): A domain ontology and thematic analysis. *Journal of Business Venturing, 26*(6), 632–659.

Jones, M. V., & Coviello, N. E. (2005). Internationalisation: Conceptualising an entrepreneurial process of behaviour in time. *Journal of International Business Studies, 36*, 284–303.

Madsen, T., & Servais, P. (1997). The internationalization of born globals: An evolutionary process? *International Business Review, 6*(6), 561–583.

McDougall, P., & Oviatt, B. (2000). International entrepreneurship: The intersection of two research paths. *Academy of Management Journal, 43*(5), 902–906.

McDougall, P. P., Shane, S., & Oviatt, B. M. (1994). Explaining the formation of international new ventures: The limits of theories from international business research. *Journal of Business Venturing, 9*(6), 469–487.

Nicholls-Nixon, C., Cooper, A., & Woo, C. (2000). Strategic experimentation: Understanding change and performance in new ventures. *Journal of Business Venturing, 15*(5-6), 493–521.

Nike. (2024). Retrieved May 14, 2024, from https://t.ly/OuC0a

Nordström, K., & Vahlne, J.-E. (1992). Is the globe shrinking? Psychic distance and the establishment of Swedish sales subsidiaries during the last 100 years. Paper presented at the International Trade and Finance Association's Annual Conference, April 22–25, Loredo, Texas.

O'Grady, S., & Lane, H. W. (1996). The psychic distance paradox. *Journal of International Business Studies, 27*, 309–333.

Petersen, B., & Welch, L. S. (2003). International business development and the internet, post-hype. *Management International Review, 43*(1), 7–29.

Prahalad, C. K. (2004). The blinders of dominant logic. *Long Range Planning, 37*(2), 171–179.

Procter & Gamble. (2017). Annual report. Retrieved March 3, 2020, from https://t.ly/xzjvE

Root, F. (1994). *Entry strategies for international markets*. Lexington Books.

Ross, J., & Staw, B. (1993). Organizational escalation and exit: Lessons from the Shoreham nuclear power plant. *Academy of Management Journal, 36*(4), 701–732.

Saarnio, A. (2016). Jolla tablet: Aiming for closure. Retrieved March 20, 2024 from https://t.ly/kPEGP

Sailfish. (2024). Retrieved March 17, 2024, from https://t.ly/nbyrP

Scott, W. R. (2013). *Institutions and organizations: Ideas, interests, and identities*. Sage Publications.

SEC. (2018). P&G acquires the consumer health business of Merck KGaA, Darmstadt, Germany. Retrieved March 4, 2024 from https://t.ly/s0ZWh

Techcrunch. (2015). Mobile OS maker Jolla to cut half its staff, restructure its debt after funding stalls. Retrieved March 17, 2024 from https://t.ly/4oaYT

Turcan, R. V. (2003). De-internationalization and the small firm. In C. Wheeler, F. McDonald, & I. Greaves (Eds.), *Internationalization: Firms strategies and management* (pp. 208–222). Palgrave.

Turcan, R. V. (2006). De-internationalization of small high-technology firms: An international entrepreneurship perspective. Doctoral dissertation, University of Strathclyde, Glasgow, UK.

Turcan, R. V. (2013). The philosophy of turning points: A case of de-internationalization. *Advances in International Management, 26*, 219–235.

Vahlne, J. E., & Johanson, J. (2020). The Uppsala model: Networks and micro-foundations. *Journal of International Business Studies, 51*(1), 4–10.

Welch, L. S., & Luostarinen, R. (1988). Internationalization: Evolution of a concept. *Journal of General Management, 14*(2), 34–55.

Welch, L. S., & Luostarinen, R. K. (1993). Inward-outward connections in internationalization. *Journal of International Marketing, 1*(1), 44–56.

Young, S., Hamill, J., Wheeler, C., & Davies, L. R. (1989). *International market entry and development: Strategies and management.* Harvester Wheatsheaf.

CHAPTER 3

De-internationalization

> *Water, water, everywhere,*
> *And all the boards did shrink;*
> *Water, water, everywhere,*
> *Nor any drop to drink.*
> —Samuel Taylor Coleridge

3.1 Swimming Toward Calm Waters

While internationalization appeals to many entrepreneurs, CEOs, investors, and policy makers as a successful and/or desired endeavor, leading to and/or stimulating growth,[1] de-internationalization, on the other hand, is perceived as a failure, an undesired enterprise. These stakeholders commit to the internationalization of diverse types of resources, e.g., physical, financial, social, and human capital; time; and reputation. Just acknowledging, never mind acting on, the need to de-commit these and other resources that were assembled and deployed to support internationalization to de-internationalize is seen as accepting and succumbing to failure. It is in human nature to suppress the admission of failure,[2] hence the perpetual (need to) focus and emphasis on "positive" international growth and persistent disregard of the importance of de-internationalization to the overall cross-border activity of the firm. Focusing only on positive or successful factors, as perceived by key stakeholders, and prescribing them as normative is akin to advising or prescribing that winning in gambling, say on horse racing, is both good and desirable—an advice solely based on people who won money on that gambling (received net gain). By adopting this approach to decision and policy making, key stakeholders risk accepting such behaviors and factors as indicators of success, when, in fact, they may be the very factors that increase the risk of failure.[3]

De-internationalization should not be viewed a priori as a failure.[4] Instead, as we advocate in this book, de-internationalization along with its "siblings," internationalization and re-internationalization, should be considered holistically part of the "*cross-border activity*" of the firm. This view would allow decision and policy makers to acknowledge, embrace, and encourage de-internationalization rather than ignore and/or avoid it to allow firms to maximize growth opportunities in domestic and international markets.[5] The questions then that most need to be addressed by entrepreneurs, CEOs, investors, and policy makers are "to what extent is the chosen mode continuing to deliver returns and positive performance, and if less than optimal, what change would better effect attainment of projected targets."[6] Understanding the why, how, what, when, who, and where of de-internationalization (Fig. 1.2) would contribute to a better understanding of internationalization, in particular, and the cross-border activity of the firm, in general. This chapter unpacks these concerns.

3.2 Defining De-internationalization

3.2.1 *Taken for Granted*

In Chap. 1, we took the first steps toward defining de-internationalization as a necessary and indispensable component of a firm's cross-border activity. Such ontological definition allows us to mitigate ubiquitous misconstructions of the relationship between internationalization, de-internatio nalization, and re-internationalization in the IB literature. For example, the following conceptualization statements are typical in IB literature:[7]

- *There are cycles of de-internationalization and re-internationalization, the antecedents, and motivators for the internationalization pathways;*

- *Internationalization, de-internationalization, and re-internationalization are separate elements in the internationalization process;*
- *De-internationalization is an important part of a firm's internationalization.*

Such erroneous misconstruction or mis-conceptualization of "internationalization, de-internationalization and re-internationalization" as part of "internationalization" is surprising because Benito and Welch's definition (which we discuss below) suggests that de-internationalization is part of firms' *cross-border* activities.[8] In this book, we adopt the view that internationalization, de-internationalization, and re-internationalization are *distinct* types of *cross-border* activities of firms[9] and apply it to analyze how BMI can help enhance our understanding of the relationship between de-internationalization and re-internationalization.

The first definition of de-internationalization conceptualizes it as "any voluntary or forced *actions* that *reduce* a firm's *engagement* in or *exposure* to current *cross-border* activities" [10] (emphasis added). This definition poses three main concerns that are embedded in the emphasized constructs *actions, reduce, engagement, exposure,* and *cross-border*. First, IB researchers take these constructs at face value, for granted, usually citing earlier research without engaging in problematization[11] of these or other assumptions that underlie de-internationalization.[12] Second, such "taking-for-grantedness" contributes to various semantic and theoretical misconceptions in defining and positioning de-internationalization and re-internationalization within IB.[13] And third, we view these constructs as critical for the process of defining and positioning de-internationalization within IB (and, within the scope of this book, within BMI).

3.2.2 Understanding Its Key Concerns

The concerns or challenges that the construct *reduce* poses for IB researchers are manifold. Indeed, a firm's *engagement* in or *exposure* to international or cross-border activities may be *reduced* due to de-internationalization. However, de-internationalization may also lead to an increase in a firm's engagement in or exposure to cross-border activities[14] or new innovation activities,[15] eventually contributing to an increase in the overall, including international, firm growth. If invalidly conceptualized as part of "internationalization," it is expected for the firm's engagement in or exposure to "internationalization" to diminish as a result of de-internationalization, contributing, inter alia, to the perception of de-internationalization as a negative and undesirable phenomenon as discussed earlier.

Such perceived negative properties of de-internationalization as these make it undesirable or inconvenient to research and regulate, producing sample selection bias when only successful firms are analyzed and receive policy support.[16] This bias dominates not only IB research but also policy making. When de-internationalization is understood and embraced by key stakeholders as part of the cross-border activity of the firm, its impact on the overall firm performance and growth is seen holistically, encouraged, and supported, for example, to pursue new international opportunities (e.g., by re-internationalizing) or new opportunities in the home market (e.g., by trade in value-added).[17]

The *action* construct poses further challenges and critical questions not only for IB researchers but also for practitioners. What kind of actions or engagements do firms employ to de-internationalize? Are they the same as the ones used to internationalize? Is de-internationalization a reverse, mirror image of internationalization? Apart from being voluntary or forced,[18] are de-internationalization actions strategic, planned, innovative, entrepreneurial, improvised, or imitative? Is it possible to explain de-internationalization (and why not re-internationalization) choices using the same, original internationalization postures?

As we highlighted in the previous chapter, commitment is one of the key dimensions of a firm's cross-border activity. Within the scope of the above queries, a key question decision-makers may (for example) ask is whether the commitment to de-internationalize is the same as it was to internationalize. The "whys" or rationale of internationalization—as part of the internationalization pattern—play a crucial role in shaping the commitment to internationalization. Having internationalized, firms expect to gain flexibility in their operations; enhance the quality of their product and services; achieve greater efficiency in production, R&D, and use of infrastructure; optimize transportation, coordination, and labor costs; and access qualified talent. These are among the primary reasons for internationalization. Interestingly, as the evidence suggests, *firms de-internationalize for the same reasons as they internationalize* (Vignette 3.1).

> **Vignette 3.1   A sameness of internationalization and de-internationalization reasons**
> Over the last 10 years, the reasons for de-internationalization remain largely unchanged. This is exemplified by the results of the longitudinal, European Manufacturing survey that the Fraunhofer Institute for Systems and Innovation Research conducts.[19] For example, based on the 2022 survey results, loss of flexibility (55%), failure to guarantee and/or maintain product and service quality (51%), and inefficient utilization of production capacity (42%) are the main reasons for firms to withdraw from international markets. High and continuously rising transportation (24%), coordination (22%), and labor (15%) costs also drive firms away from their international markets. Increasing labor cost might be an opportunity to attract highly qualified personnel locally; however, lack of qualified personnel (13%) adds to firms' dissatisfaction with their international presence. Other de-internationalization drivers include lack of infrastructure (11%), vicinity of R&D at home (5%), and know-how loss (2%).

This "conundrum" begs many questions. For example, how was it possible for a firm to internationalize in the first place? Was internationalization an error? How to justify de-internationalization (e.g., "we have internationalized five years ago to become more flexible, enhance the quality of our product and services, achieve greater economy of scale and scope, and optimize our operational, production, and labor costs. Now, we have to withdraw from this market as none of the above was successfully achieved")? Is or can de-internationalization be an *error-correction mechanism*?[20] How to de-internationalize, considering the same reasons but different commitments between internationalization and de-internatio nalization?

3.2.3   *Constructing Its Domain*

The inverse relationship between the two commitments defines the relationship between internationalization and de-internationalization: as the firm's commitment to its internationalization increases, the probability of de-internationalizing decreases.[21] Oftentimes, an increased commitment

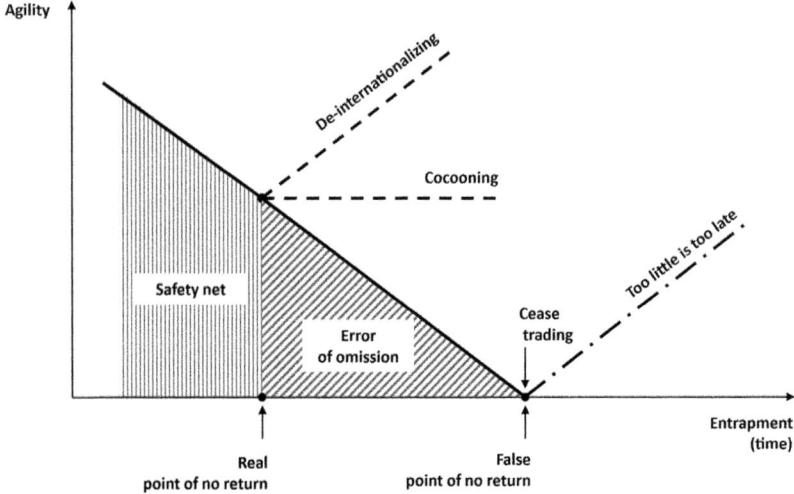

Fig. 3.1 De-internationalization as a turning point

to internationalization (or to any other actions with a high project, psychological, social, and organizational commitments that are at stake)[22] acts as a trap,[23] a blinder,[24] or an entrapment,[25] discouraging the firm to de-internationalize. At the same time, an entrapment to a failing course of action diminishes the firm's agility; these relationships are depicted in Fig. 3.1.[26]

Firms may not only end up entrapped, "*drifting idly towards eternity, but they can reach a point of 'no return', where they have become so run down as to be almost financially worthless.*"[27] They may lose their agility, defined as "*flexible decision making and a flexible cost base structure that allow decision makers … to scale up and more importantly to scale down according to the activity level that the firm is experiencing.*"[28] In such a situation, one of the key questions to ask is when it is not too late to de-internationalize? When to "pull the plug" and return home?

As an error-correction mechanism, de-internationalization can mitigate two types of errors: *an error of commission* (De-e1), which is when a firm should not have de-internationalized earlier but did so; and/or *an error of omission* (De-e2), which is when a firm should have de-internationalized earlier but failed to do so.[29] "Pulling the plug" too early (De-e1), firms may lose ongoing opportunities in the international markets. "Pulling the plug" too late (De-e2) may allow the firms to recover and even re-internationalize, but withdrawing too late may result in the firm's failure, risking, in some cases, even complete bankruptcy.

One of the main challenges, if not the key one, in deciding when to change the trajectory or the course of the firm from internationalization to de-internationalization is to "estimate," "see," and "feel" the *turning point* between the two trajectories. What firms need to define as accurately as possible is the *real point of no return*, a point in a firm's life beyond which the existing organizational gestalt is insufficient to support the transition to a new viable gestalt.[30] Before the "real point of no return," even when "committing too early," the firm has a reasonable *safety net*, a chance not only to survive but also to move from initial cross-border equilibrium to a new one by "equilibrium adjustment" de-internationalization[31] (see Fig. 3.1). The firm "pulling the plug" too close to the "real point of no return" may still have a minimum *safety net* that could offer a chance to "turn around" and change (maybe successfully) its cross-border trajectory. Within this proximity, the firm may decide to adopt *cocooning* as its de-internationalization business model: "to go into hibernation, survive the worst of the winter, close down the essential organs, and keep alive, so that when the spring comes you can open up again"[32] (see also Vignette 4.1). In this context, *de-internationalization* is defined as "*the firm's capacity to [reconfigure its] organizational gestalt before or at the real point of no return.*"[33]

Due to its dominant, internationalization, logic, or escalating commitment to a failing course of action that can act as a trap or a blinder, the firm can estimate incorrectly its real turning point, thinking and/or believing it has time and resources to successfully de-internationalize. As a result, what the firm defines is a *false turning point*, an illusionary point of no return that is the result of the process of illusion and self-deception; a difference between real and false points of no return is *error of omission* (De-e2).[34] If the firm is not agile enough to see its real point of no return, get entrapped in or continue its commitment to internationalization that is failing or not optimal, it will "commit" to a false point of no return, believing it's real, then any of its decisions to de-internationalize will not be successful and will lead to failure.

De-internationalization is a complex process indeed, taking myriad shapes and forms. It can be (voluntary) or forced;[35] fast or slow; successful

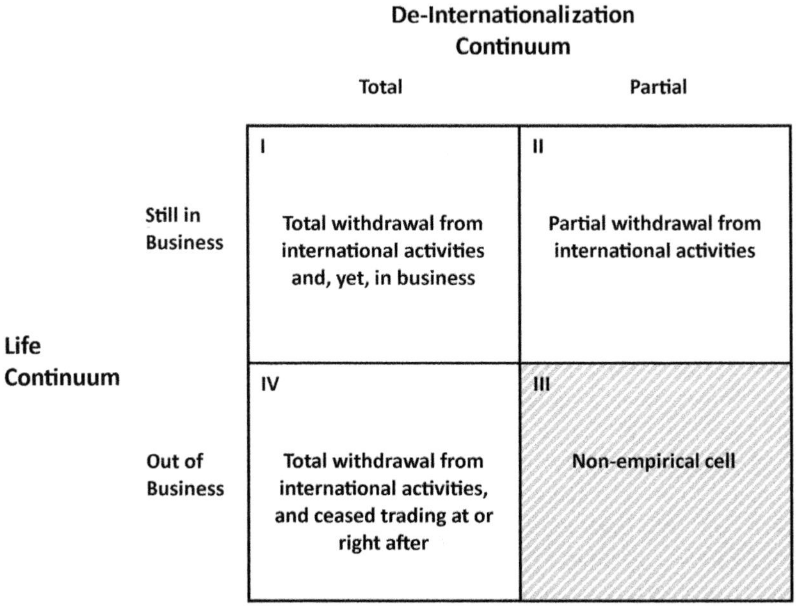

	De-Internationalization Continuum	
	Total	**Partial**
Still in Business	**I** Total withdrawal from international activities and, yet, in business	**II** Partial withdrawal from international activities
Out of Business	**IV** Total withdrawal from international activities, and ceased trading at or right after	**III** Non-empirical cell

(Life Continuum — vertical axis)

Fig. 3.2 The typology of de-internationalization

(still in business) or unsuccessful (failure or out of business); strategic or entrepreneurial; positive or negative; total or partial; innovative or business-as-usual; dependent or independent; direct or indirect; real or false. Iterating[36] these external and internal concepts, properties, and indicators of de-internationalization led to the emergence of a *comprehensive* and *parsimonious*[37] set of factors that were employed to develop a *typology of de-internationalization* (Fig. 3.2).[38] These factors were the de-internationalization continuum (total vs. partial) and firm life continuum (in business vs. out of business).

Cross-tabulating these factors generated three types of de-internationalization.[39] *Total withdrawal* or de-internationalization (Quadrant I): firms in this quadrant withdraw totally from international markets and focus entirely on serving their domestic markets and/or continue serving international markets via indirect exporting or by trade in value added.[40] *Partial withdrawal* or de-internationalization (Quadrant II): firms in this quadrant remain active internationally, but may have switched to lower risk, cost, and commitment mode of entry or relocated their production and/or service to closer-to-home markets—physically or psychically. An *extreme case of total withdrawal* or de-internationalization (Quadrant IV): firms in this quadrant cease trading at or shortly after de-internationalization. Quadrant III is a non-empirical cell,[41] as firms in this quadrant logically cannot exist.

3.3 The "whys" of De-internationalization

External and internal factors urge firms to de-internationalize[42] (Table 3.1).[43] Examples of macro, micro, and cultural factors as external drivers of de-internationalization include changes in national legal and normative environments, such as exchange rates, tariffs, inflation, and ownership structures; cultural differences and physical distance; maturity of the offer in the target market; increased attractiveness of the home or close-to-home markets; increased production and transportation costs; quality and availability of labor; and collaboration constraints with low quality or performance of value chain partners, such as original equipment manufacturers (OEMs), venture capitalists (VCs), suppliers, and distributors (see also Vignette 4.1).

Table 3.1 The "whys" of de-internationalization

External factors
Changes in national legal and normative environments
Collaboration constraints (OEMs and VCs)
Cultural difference/physical distance
Increased attractiveness of the home market
Increased production and transportation costs
Lack in or poor performance of suppliers or distributors
Quality and availability of labor
Quality of partners
Market opportunity disappearance
Internal factors
Change in ownership
Decreased quality/profitability of the offer
Intangible assets (both quality and quantity)
Lack of innovation
Lack of international experience
Lack of technological/technical capabilities
New, more efficient production/technology
Underperforming subsidiaries
Maturity of the product in the target market

Speed of internationalization, product diversification, corporate governance and ownership, poor subsidiary performance, decreased offer quality, lack of international experience, and lack of technological and technical capabilities are examples of internal factors that lead firms to de-internationalize (see also Vignette 4.1). Innovation—as a double-edged sword—is also identified as an internal driver. A lack of innovation can influence a firm's decision to de-internationalize. At the same time, successful innovation, e.g., resulting in more efficient production and technology automation, can press firms to de-internationalization.

As we have highlighted in the "Understanding its key concerns" section above, the main, most frequent external and internal factors that drive firms to de-internationalize are the same drivers that motivate firms to internationalize. To the list of questions we have identified, we can add one more to aid researchers and practitioners to shed some light on this "conundrum." When an activity or phenomenon is perceived as "negative," as de-internationalization is, people tend to take credit for positive outcomes and *attribute* negative outcomes to external factors, no matter what their true cause is. The question is how to mitigate and/or control for such "attribution errors"[44] within the scope of this internationalization–de-internationalization paradox? Particularly, in the case of advanced internationalization (e.g., via joint ventures, acquisitions, and greenfield investments), understanding the impact of the autonomy of a subsidiary and/or the relationship between headquarters and subsidiaries on attribution errors before, during, and after de-internationalization is pivotal to overall firm growth.

3.4 The "hows" of De-internationalization

How firms de-internationalize depends considerably on how they are internationalized. Specifically, it depends on the level of commitment to risk, cost, and control initially or subsequently undertaken to an entry mode, along with associated project, psychological, social, and organizational embeddedness. For example, to totally de-internationalize (Quadrant I, Fig. 3.2), closing a sales subsidiary can be much easier than closing an R&D or production subsidiary. In the pursuit of the same aim, closing a firm's own sales subsidiary can be much easier than closing a joint-venture sales subsidiary. Having reached home, the outputs (e.g., withdrawing costs and salvage value) and outcomes (e.g., success or failure) of respective de-internationalization will affect future re-internationalization efforts of the firm, provided these will not cause the firm to cease to exist.

The higher the commitment to initial or subsequent internationalization, the bigger the distance—geographical, operational, and/or psychological—the firm must cover "swimming towards calm waters" (assuming the correctly estimated real point of no return; otherwise, guided by a false point of no return, it will most likely perish). Whether the identified "calm waters" are new, alternative internal markets or the home market, the firms can de-internationalize by optimizing their exit modes, international markets, or operations (Fig. 3.3).[45]

A firm that partly withdraws from a foreign market can optimize (1) its operations in that market,[46] (2) the number of entered foreign markets,[47] or (3) entry modes, switching to the modes that entail a lesser risk, cost, or control.[48] A firm may optimize its foreign markets by backshoring, off-shoring, near-shoring, or re-shoring;[49] friend-shoring;[50] decoupling;[51] or re-coupling. It may also optimize its operations in a foreign market

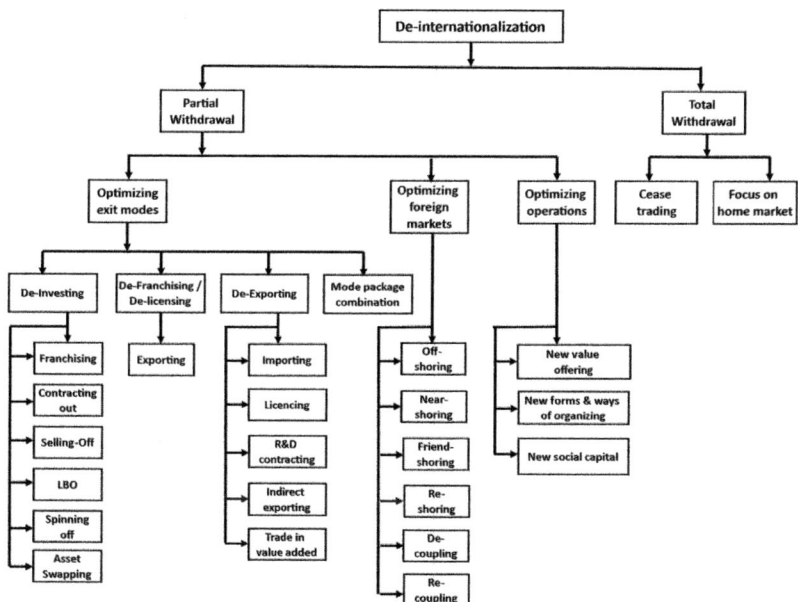

Fig. 3.3 The "hows" of de-internationalization

through a new value offering, ways or forms of organizing, or social capital.[52] Further zooming into the "hows" the firm may consider between de-internationalization of ownership or de-internationalization of control,[53] a firm may decide to de-invest, de-franchise, or de-export. De-investment can be achieved through franchising, contracting out, selling out, leveraged buy-out, spin-off, or asset swap.[54] From franchising (or licensing), a firm may switch, for example, to exporting,[55] and from exporting to importing, licensing in, research and development (R&D) contracting,[56] indirect exporting, and trade in added value.[57] Often firms have a combination of entry modes, or mode packages, serving a single market or several markets. Firms may optimize their mode packages to "de-emphasize,"[58] for example, a change from a joint venture to a combined mode of licensing and exporting.

3.5 Special Cases of De-internationalization

A special case can be defined by a *critical event*, new theoretical lens, or new context. An event is critical if it deviates positively or negatively from what is normal or expected. The behavior of special cases as one might expect is atypical. Studying these cases is of critical importance not only for academics but also for practitioners and policy makers. In the context of de-internationalization, examples of such special cases include, for example, Russia's war against Ukraine and the advanced internationalization of universities.

The Russian against Ukraine is a critical event. The behavior of firms after the start of the war in February 2022 revealed new, fine-grained modes of de-internationalization that were either not present or not observable during operations in normal, business-as-usual times and enhanced the conceptualization and understanding of the existing modes of de-internationalization (Vignette 3.2). These are:[59]

- *Withdrawal*: clean break, surgical removal [complete withdrawal, QI in Fig. 3.3];
- *Suspension*: keeping options open for return (firms temporarily curtailing most or nearly all operations while keeping return options open) [partial withdrawal, QII in Fig. 3.3];
- *Scaling back*: reducing current operations (scaling back some significant business operations but continuing some others) [partial withdrawal, QII in Fig. 3.3];

- *Buying time*: holding off new investments/development (firms postponing future planned investment/development/marketing while continuing substantive business) [partial withdrawal, QII in Fig. 3.3];
- *Digging in*: defying demands for exit or reduction of activities (firms that are just continuing business-as-usual in Russia).

Vignette 3.2 De-internationalization of firms from Russia

As Russia's war against Ukraine started in 2022, it strained the relation between Russia and Western countries, leading to sanctions against Russia imposed by the European Union, the United States, and other nations, e.g., sanctions on the economy, individuals, firms, institutions, and specific sectors (arms, energy, and banks).[60]

Many Western firms facing the reality had to make decisions regarding their ongoing operations in Russia. For example, several American firms either *scaled back* their operations or completely *withdrew* from Russia. A notable example is Yum! Brands, the owner of KFC, Pizza Hut, and Taco Bell. Its exit strategy involved de-investment and de-franchising of its operations to a local franchisee, a complete exit of ownership and operational control. For example, it sold its entire KFC business, over 1000 restaurants, to Smart Service Ltd., a local operator. It also involved de-exporting by stopping the supply chain flow of ingredients and operational resources.[61]

McDonald's and Starbucks chose a strategy of de-investment and de-operation by temporarily closing and withdrawing their investments and ongoing operations. Coca-Cola and PepsiCo adopted de-exporting strategies, where both chose to halt their Russian production plants and suspend their operations.[62]

Within the automobile industry, it is worth mentioning the de-exporting strategy of GM, that suspended their production/operations supply in their manufacturing plant in St. Petersburg as part of their global restructuring plan, and Ford Motor's de-investment strategy, that announced its intention to exit the Russian market through a joint venture sale by transferring operational control and ownership to Sollers.[63]

What makes a university, pursuing *advanced structural internationalization*, a special case is the adoption of a new theoretical lens to understand its advanced structural internationalization, such as joint ventures, acquisitions, or green or brownfield investments. When a university pursues such activities, academics, practitioners, and policy makers "treat" them as any other, typical, multinational enterprise and study and regulate them accordingly by applying same theoretical, IB lenses. For example, a typical question within the scope of IB is "whether the organization and values a university espouses at home can be transferred as-is or adapted to the foreign country in the pursuit of 'advanced structural' internationalization."[64] However, from a different theoretical perspective, *university autonomy*, an unlikely conjecture emerges about the effect of such activity on a university. Namely, that transferring as-is or adapting the organization and values of a university in the pursuit of advanced structural internationalization "neither is viable nor ethical."[65]

Regardless of such worrisome signals, universities do engage in advanced structural internationalization. In the last two decades, lucrative, primarily financial, motives have driven advanced structural internationalization of universities from North America and Europe into emerging countries. Advanced structural internationalization of university is "legitimated by the argument that the parent institution's brand is a guarantee that the transplanted institution is part of a global higher education elite, providing world-class education."[66] However, it has not become normative. Furthermore, it triggered massive total or partial de-internationalization of universities from these markets (Table 3.2).[67] Surveying the motives (the "whys") of de-internationalization of universities, it can be observed that they follow similar patterns of de-internationalization of (usual, mainstream) firms, e.g., lack of due diligence before internationalizing.

Special cases, such as these, also reveal common patterns otherwise unobservable or perceived as not critical in normal, business-as-usual times. For example, the role of ethics in doing business or the impact of business on ethics. Critical events and contexts, new theoretical lenses offer opportunities to fully appreciate the impact and the role of ethics.

3.6 Concluding Remarks

Embracing "de-internationalization" is an intricate process. It requires decision-makers to invest in changing how de-internationalization is *perceived*, externally and internally, by the key stakeholders of the firm and in *understanding* it, as well as what is required to act on it. Defining and conceptualizing it as a part of a cross-border activity of the firm will help

Table 3.2 De-internationalization of universities

University	Entry strategy	Entry	Exit	De-internationalization type	The "whys" of de-internationalization
Royal Melbourne Institute of Technology (Malaysia)	Joint venture: Adorna Institute of Technology is created as a joint venture with Adorna property developers	1996	1999	Partial de-internationalization: having learned the importance of a reliable financial base and realistic assessments of student demand, it went on to establish two successful branch campuses in Vietnam; *total de-investment*	Change in the local environment/a critical event: economic crisis in Southeast Asia. Local partner was hard hit by the crisis
Central Queensland University (Fiji)	Branch campus formation as greenfield investment	1998	2007	Partial de-internationalization: the university restructured its international activities; today has a single TNE partner in the delivery of offshore programs (Melior International College, Singapore); *total de-investment*	Change in the local environment/a critical event: sudden change in local socio-political climate, instability. Declining international enrollments
George Mason University (UAE, Ras al-Khaimah)	Branch campus established as a joint venture with the local government. Received considerable subsidies and funding	2005	2009	Total de-internationalization, staying in business, focusing on internationalization at home; *Total de-investment*	Low enrollment numbers. Poor conditions: failure to finish campus buildings on time. Limited curriculum options. Funding difficulties: 50% reduction in the promised subsidies for the venture. Poor communication: disagreements with local partners, failing to agree on funding levels with RAK Government. Unfavorable location

(*continued*)

Table 3.2 (continued)

University	Entry strategy	Entry	Exit	De-internationalization type	The "whys" of de-internationalization
University of New South Wales (Singapore)	Branch campus, sponsored by the local government	2007	2007	Total de-internationalization (after four months of operation), staying in business, focusing on internationalization at home; *total de-investment*	Low enrollment numbers High tuition fees, high entry standards, failure to understand the student market Starting as a large comprehensive venture Funding problems Strong local competition Geographical proximity of the mother institution
Tisch Asia, a branch of New York University (Singapore)	Branch campus, partially funded by the local government	2007	2014	Partial de-internationalization, more focus on the activities of the Global network University operating international branches in Shanghai and Abu Dhabi; *total de-investment*	Slow enrollment growth Very high tuition fees, difficulty attracting local students Unsustainable subject for the local market and lack of supportive (creative) industries Reluctance to hire local academics Internal issues: disagreements between the headquarters and the branch Financial challenges, funding problems: reduction of subsidies by the hosting government

Michigan State University (UAE, Dubai)	Branch campus, partially funded by the local government	2008	2010	Total de-internationalization, staying in business, focusing on internationalization at home; *total de-investment*	Very high tuition fees Slow enrollment growth Limited curriculum options Competition with other full-size branch campuses in the region Dubai's economic crisis
University of Waterloo (UAE campus)	Branch campus created as a joint venture with the United Arab Emirates Higher Colleges of Technology	2009	2012	Partial de-internationalization: Waterloo International keeps looking for opportunities in the UAE, continues internationalizing through partnerships, and foreign offices (Hong-Kong office, Sino-Canadian college); *partial de-investment*	Study programs were not as lucrative as anticipated Slow enrollment growth Financial uncertainty Traditional mission and vision Insufficient research linkages Focus on undergraduate education

to mitigate any negative perceptions or views toward de-internationalization. This, in turn, will urge key stakeholders to acknowledge, embrace, and encourage de-internationalization rather than ignore and/or avoid it. The three frameworks that we introduced here, *de-internationalization as a turning point*, *de-internationalization typology*, and *de-internationalization modes* (the "hows") will facilitate decision-makers' understanding of de-internationalization. The first highlights the timing of de-internationalization commitment and defines possible consequences of misaligning the timing, commitment, and configurations of organizational gestalt and de-internationalization decisions. De-internationalization typology, defining the three types of de-internationalization, assists decision-makers in understanding possible outcomes of de-internationalization to further reconfigure the organizational gestalt of the firm, for example, for the purpose of re-internationalization. The latter offers, not exhaustively, a set of de-internationalization modes that decision-makers could consider as part of partial or total withdrawal strategy. Opportunities to advance our understanding of de-internationalization emerge when a phenomenon can be defined as a critical event, studied in new contexts, and/or via new theories as we showed with two special cases, the Russian war against Ukraine and advanced structural internationalization of universities.

Notes

1. "The role and impact of internationalization on firm performance remains elusive and inconclusive. The IB theories on one side assume a positive relationship between internationalization and firm performance. On the other side, the empirical evidence suggests the opposite, internationalization cannot be considered in general as a high-growth strategy. Instead, the "average MNE" is slow-growing in terms of quantitative and qualitative growth and struggling year by year to keep the operating margin above the break-even point. It is concluded that MNEs are more pulled into internationalization instead of pushing this process. However, at a certain firm size level, the only way to grow further is to internationalize but at the cost of profitability" (Wehrmann, 2018, p. 3).
2. Clarke and Gall (1987).
3. Davidsson (2003).
4. Crick (2004), Pauwels and Matthyssens (1999).
5. Turcan (2006).
6. Turcan (2003, p. 217).

7. These quotes are slightly modified, without changing the meaning, to avoid the possibility of identifying the authors and/or their respective publications.
8. Benito and Welch (1997); the same view is also found in work by Calof and Beamish (1995), Turcan (2003, 2006) and Welch and Luostarinen (1988).
9. Turcan (2003, 2006).
10. Benito and Welch (1997, p. 9).
11. Alvesson and Sandberg (2011).
12. For an exception, see Turcan (2006).
13. Turcan (2006).
14. For example, Chen et al. (2019), Turcan (2006).
15. Kumar (2020).
16. Turcan et al. (2010).
17. OECD (2023).
18. Benito and Welch (1997).
19. Dachs and Zanker (2014), Dachs et al. (2019), ISI (2022).
20. Casson (1986).
21. Benito and Welch (1997), Turcan (2006).
22. Drummond (1994), Ross and Staw (1993).
23. Chesbrough (2003).
24. Prahalad (2004).
25. Drummond (2004), Turcan (2013).
26. Turcan (2006, 2013).
27. Drummond (2004, p. 487).
28. Turcan (2008, p. 295).
29. Casson (1986).
30. Turcan (2006, 2013).
31. Casson (1986).
32. Turcan (2006).
33. Turcan (2006).
34. Turcan (2006, 2013).
35. Benito and Welch (1997).
36. It was based on Glaser's (1978) method of constructing typologies.
37. Comprehensiveness asks whether all relevant factors are included in the new theory and parsimony—whether some factors should be deleted because they add little additional value to the new theory (Whetten, 1989).
38. Turcan (2006).
39. In Chap. 6, we link these types of de-internationalization with BMI value drivers.
40. OECD (2023).
41. Glaser (1978).

42. Benito and Welch (1997), Bernini et al. (2016), Kafouros et al. (2022), Leonidou et al. (2018), Meneses and Pinho (2019), Tang et al. (2021), Turcan (2006), Welch and Welch (2009).
43. A thematic review of 218 de-internationalization articles by Tang et al. (2021) offered a view of these drivers. For our book, we (1) purposefully selected empirical papers from several review papers to identify external and internal drivers of de-internationalization and (2) focused only on recent (from 2000) empirical papers. Note: these empirical papers were purposefully sampled from Bernini et al. (2016), Kafouros et al. (2022), Meneses and Pinho (2019), Tang et al. (2021), and Turcan (2006).
44. Lovallo and Kahneman (2003, p. 57).
45. Derived from Turcan (2006), Sort and Turcan (2019), and Sort et al. (2023) and enhanced and revised for the purpose and scope of this book.
46. Tan and Sousa (2018).
47. Papyrina (2007).
48. Palmer and Quinn (2007).
49. Bals et al. (2015), Buckley (2023), Dachs et al. (2019), De Backer et al. (2016), Ellram (2013), Mondres (2022), UNCTAD (2013).
50. Javorcik et al. (2024).
51. Buckley (2023), Cui et al. (2023), Li (2021), Vertinsky et al. (2023), Witt et al. (2023).
52. Kumar and Srivastava (2020); Mellahi (2003), Palmer and Quinn (2007), Pauwels and Matthyssens (1999), Turcan (2006), Turner and Gardiner (2007).
53. For example, Casson (1986).
54. Berry (2013), Coyne and Wright (1986), Mohr et al. (2018), Soule et al. (2014).
55. Fraser (2001).
56. Bernini et al. (2016), Chen et al. (2019), Crick (2004), Pauwels and Matthyssens (1999).
57. OECD (2018).
58. Benito et al. (2009, p. 1461).
59. Sonnenfeld et al. (2022); as of March, 2024, 215 firms were "digging in," 175 "buying time," 154 "scaling back," 504 "suspending," and 541 "withdrawing" their operations in/from Russia (CELI 2024).
60. European Council (2024), US Department of State (2024).
61. Yum (2023), Food and Wine (2022).
62. McDonald's (2022), Starbucks Stories & News (2022), Coca-Cola (2022), PepsiCo (2022).
63. GM (2024), Ford (2022), The Moscow Times (2022).

64. Turcan et al. (2021).
65. Turcan et al. (2021).
66. Turcan et al. (2021).
67. Turcan and Gulieva (2016, p. 319).

References

Alvesson, M., & Sandberg, J. (2011). Generating research questions through problematization. *Academy of Management Review, 36*(2), 247–271.

Bals, L., Anika, D., & Wendy, T. (2015). From offshoring to rightshoring: Focus on the backshoring phenomenon. *AIB Insights, 15*(4), 3–8.

Benito, G., & Welch, L. (1997). De-internationalization. *Management International Review, 37*, 7–25.

Benito, G. R., Petersen, B., & Welch, L. S. (2009). Towards more realistic conceptualisations of foreign operation modes. *Journal of International Business Studies, 40*, 1455–1470.

Bernini, M., Du, J., & Love, J. H. (2016). Explaining intermittent exporting: Exit and conditional re-entry in export markets. *Journal of International Business Studies, 47*(9), 1058–1076.

Berry, H. (2013). When do firms divest foreign operations? *Organization Science, 24*(1), 246–261.

Buckley, P. J. (2023). Corporate reactions to the fracturing of the global economy. *International Business Review, 32*(6).

Calof, J. L., & Beamish, P. W. (1995). Adapting to foreign markets: Explaining internationalization. *International Business Review, 4*(2), 115–131.

Casson, M. (1986). International divestment and restructuring decisions: With special reference to the motor industry. *International Labour Organization*. Working Paper 40.

CELI. (2024). Over 1,000 companies have curtailed operations in Russia—but some remain. Retrieved March 5, 2024 from https://t.ly/7Mztg

Chen, J., Sousa, C. M., & He, X. (2019). Export market re-entry: Time-out period and price/quality dynamisms. *Journal of World Business, 54*(2), 154–168.

Chesbrough, H. (2003). *Open innovation: The new imperative for creating and profiting from technology*. Harvard Business School Press.

Clarke, C., & Gall, F. (1987). Planned divestment – A five step approach. *Long Range Planning, 20*(1), 17–25.

Coca-Cola Company. (2022). The Coca-Cola company suspends its business in Russia. Retrieved April 22, 2024, from https://t.ly/t2nGD

Coyne, J., & Wright, M. (1986). An introduction to divestment: The conceptual issues. In J. Coyne & M. Wright (Eds.), *Divestment and strategic change* (pp. 1–26). Philip Allan Publishers.

Crick, D. (2004). U.K. SMEs' decision to discontinue exporting: An exploratory investigation into practices within the clothing industry. *Journal of Business Venturing*, *19*(4), 561–587.

Cui, V., Vertinsky, I., & Wang, Y. (2023). Decoupling in international business: The "new" vulnerability of globalization and MNEs' response strategies. *Journal of International Business Studies*, *54*, 1562–1576.

Dachs, B., Kinkel, S., & Jäger, A. (2019). Bringing it all back home? Backshoring of manufacturing activities and the adoption of Industry 4.0 technologies. *Journal of World Business*, *54*(6), 1–15.

Dachs, B., & Zanker, C. (2014). Backshoring of production activities in European manufacturing. *European Manufacturing Survey*. Retrieved May 2021, from https://t.ly/jDaqN

Davidsson, P. (2003). What entrepreneurship research can do for business and policy practice. *International Journal of Entrepreneurship Education*, *1*(1), 5–24.

De Backer, K., Menon, C., Desnoyers-James, I., & Moussiegt, L. (2016). *Reshoring: Myth or reality?* OECD.

Drummond, H. (1994). Too little too late: A case study of escalation in decision making. *Organization Studies*, *15*(4), 591–607.

Drummond, H. (2004). See you next week? A study of entrapment in a small business. *International Small Business Journal*, *22*(5), 487–502.

Ellram, L. M. (2013). Offshoring, reshoring, and the manufacturing location decision. *Journal of Supply Chain Management*, *49*(2), 3.

European Council. (2024). EU sanctions against Russia. Retrieved April 11, 2024, from https://t.ly/Rp2JZ

Food & Wine. (2022, July 6). KFC and Pizza Hut are officially pulling out of Russia. *Food & Wine*. https://t.ly/bC0zs

Ford. (2022). Retrieved March 5, 2024 from https://t.ly/nFdg9

Fraser, L. (2001). Causes of disruption to franchise operations. *Journal of Business Research*, *54*(3), 227–234.

Glaser, B. (1978). *Theoretical sensitivity*. Sociology Press.

GM. (2024). Our path to an all-electric future: Zero crashes, zero emissions, zero congestion. Retrieved April 18, 2024, from https://t.ly/bRBq0

Javorcik, B., Kitzmueller, L., Schweiger, H., & Yıldırım, M. A. (2024). Economic costs of friendshoring. *The World Economy*, *47*(7), 2871–2908.

Kafouros, M., Cavusgil, S. T., Devinney, T. M., Ganotakis, P., & Fainshmidt, S. (2022). Cycles of de-internationalization and re-internationalization: Towards an integrative framework. *Journal of World Business*, *57*(1), 101257.

Kumar, V. (2020). Global implications of cause-related loyalty marketing. *International Marketing Review*, *37*(4), 747–772.

Kumar, V., & Srivastava, R. (2020). New perspectives on business model innovations in emerging markets. *Journal of the Academy of Marketing Science*, *48*, 815–825.

Leonidou, L. C., Katsikeas, C. S., Samiee, S., & Aykol, B. (2018). International marketing research: A state-of-the-art review and the way forward. *Advances in Global Marketing*, 3–33.

Li, P. P. (2021). The new challenges in the emerging context of global decoupling. In *Globalization, political economy, business and society in pandemic times* (pp. 221–235). Emerald Publishing Limited.

Lovallo, D., & Kahneman, D. (2003). Delusions of success. *Harvard Business Review, 81*(7), 56–63.

McDonald's. (2022, May 16). McDonald's to exit from Russia. Retrieved April 22, 2024, from https://t.ly/wm1CO

Mellahi, K. (2003). The de-internationalization process: A case study of Marks and Spencer. In *Internationalization: Firm strategies and management* (pp. 150–162). Palgrave Macmillan UK.

Meneses, R., & Pinho, H. (2019). Causes of de-internationalization: Evidence of six cases. In *Handbook of research on corporate restructuring and globalization* (pp. 170–192). IGI Global.

Mohr, A., Batsakis, G., & Stone, Z. (2018). Explaining the effect of rapid internationalization on horizontal foreign divestment in the retail sector: An extended Penrosean perspective.

Mondres, T. (2022). Onshoring, nearshoring, re-shoring: Real trend or the latest buzzwords? *American Bankers Association. ABA Banking Journal, 114*(6), 36–36.

OECD. (2018). Trade in value-added. Retrieved June 2021, from https://t.ly/Pq7az

OECD. (2023). Trade in value-added. https://t.ly/itJRz

Palmer, M., & Quinn, B. (2007). The nature of international retail divestment: Insights from Ahold. *International Marketing Review, 24*(1), 26–45.

Papyrina, V. (2007). When, how, and with what success? The joint effect of entry timing and entry mode on survival of Japanese subsidiaries in China. *Journal of International Marketing, 15*(3), 73–95.

Pauwels, P., & Matthyssens, P. (1999). A strategy process perspective on export withdrawal. *Journal of International Marketing, 7*(3), 10–37.

PepsiCo. (2022). PepsiCo suspends production & sale of Pepsi in Russia. Continues to provide essential foods. Retrieved April 22, 2024, from https://t.ly/Qvjxh

Prahalad, C. K. (2004). The blinders of dominant logic. *Long Range Planning, 37*(2), 171–179.

Ross, J., & Staw, B. (1993). Organizational escalation and exit: Lessons from the Shoreham nuclear power plant. *Academy of Management Journal, 36*(4), 701–732.

Sonnenfeld, J., Tian, S., Sokolowski, F., Wyrebkowski, M., & Kasprowicz, M. (2022, July 19). Business retreats and sanctions are crippling the Russian economy. Retrieved April 24, 2024, from https://t.ly/rz1Ad

Sort, J. C., & Turcan, R. V. (2019). De-internationalization: A business model perspective. *Journal of Business Models, 7*(4), 39–44.

Sort, J. C., Turcan, R. V., & Taran, Y. (2023). De-internationalisation, re-internationalisation and business model innovation: Exploring the intersection. *Journal of Business Models, 11*(3), 77–96.

Soule, S. A., Swaminathan, A., & Tihanyi, L. (2014). The diffusion of foreign divestment from Burma. *Strategic Management Journal, 35*(7), 1032–1052.

Starbucks. (2022). Update to Starbucks partners on our business in Russia. *Starbucks.* Retrieved April 22, 2024, from https://t.ly/Wk9OI

Tan, Q., & Sousa, C. M. (2018). Performance and business relatedness as drivers of exit decision: A study of MNCs from an emerging country. *Global Strategy Journal, 8*(4), 612–634.

Tang, R. W., Zhu, Y., Cai, H., & Han, J. (2021). De-internationalization: A thematic review and the directions forward. *Management International Review, 61*(3), 267–312.

The Moscow Times. (2022, October 27). Ford to exit Russia with joint venture sale. *The Moscow Times.* https://t.ly/Hq7JA

Turcan, R., Juho, A., & Reilly, J. (2021). Advanced structural internationalization of universities is unethical. *Organization, 28*(6), 1059–1067.

Turcan, R. V. (2003). De-internationalization and the small firm. In C. Wheeler, F. McDonald, & I. Greaves (Eds.), *Internationalization: Firms strategies and management* (pp. 208–222). Palgrave.

Turcan, R. V. (2006). De-internationalization of small high-technology firms: An international entrepreneurship perspective. Doctoral dissertation, University of Strathclyde, Glasgow, UK.

Turcan, R. V. (2008). Entrepreneur–venture capitalist relationships: Mitigating post-investment dyadic tensions. *Venture Capital, 10*(3), 281–304.

Turcan, R. V. (2013). The philosophy of turning points: A case of de-internationalization. *Advances in International Management, 26*, 219–235.

Turner, C., & Gardiner, P. D. (2007). De-internationalisation and global strategy: The case of British Telecommunications (BT). *Journal of Business & Industrial Marketing, 22*(7), 489–497.

Turcan, R. V., & Gulieva, V. (2016). De-internationalization of universities: An exploratory study. In *Finding solutions to the challenges of internationalisation* (pp. 313–329). Aalborg Universitetsforlag.

Turcan, R. V., Mäkelä, M. M., Sørensen, O. J., & Rönkkö, M. (2010). Mitigating theoretical and coverage biases in the design of theory-building research: an example from international entrepreneurship. *International Entrepreneurship and Management Journal, 6*, 399–417.

U.S. Dept. of State. (2024). Ukraine and Russia sanctions. Retrieved April 11, 2024, from https://t.ly/yn4kj

UNCTAD. (2013). *Global value chains: Investment and trade for development*. United Nations Publications. Retrieved November 2016, from https://t.ly/MbcCJ

Vertinsky, I., Kuang, Y., Zhou, D., & Cui, V. (2023). The political economy and dynamics of bifurcated world governance and the decoupling of value chains: An alternative perspective. *Journal of International Business Studies, 54*(7), 1351–1377.

Wehrmann, D. (2018). *Critical geopolitics of the polar regions: An inter-American perspective*. Routledge.

Welch, C. L., & Welch, L. S. (2009). Re-internationalization: Exploration and conceptualisation. *International Business Review, 18*(6), 567–577.

Welch, L. S., & Luostarinen, R. (1988). Internationalization: Evolution of a concept. *Journal of General Management, 14*(2), 34–55.

Whetten, D. A. (1989). What constitutes a theoretical contribution? *Academy of Management Review, 14*(4), 490–495.

Witt, M. A., Lewin, A. Y., Li, P. P., & Gaur, A. (2023). Decoupling in international business: Evidence, drivers, impact, and implications for IB research. *Journal of World Business, 58*(1).

Yum! Brands. (2023, April 17). Yum! Brands exit from Russia complete. Retrieved April 22, 2024, from https://t.ly/B08Ch

CHAPTER 4

Re-internationalization

I must go down to the sea again, to the lonely sea and the sky,
And all I ask is a tall ship and a star to steer her by,
And the wheel's kick and the wind's song and the white sail's shaking,
And a grey mist on the sea's face and a great dawn breaking.
—John Masefield

4.1 RE-CALIBRATING THE COMPASS, THE SHIP

Daedalus warned his son, Icarus, "You must follow a course midway between earth and heaven, in case the sun should scorch your feathers, if you go too high, or the water make them heavy if you are too low. Fly halfway between the two."[1] It was Icarus' eagerness for the open sky that drew him too close to the sun and, eventually, led to his demise. It could have been his enthusiasm for deep water. Icarus could have gotten too close to the water or the sun because of poor instructions or guidance; or a strong wind. Whatever the reason for getting *close* to the sun or water but yet able to recover and continue flying or *too close*, passing a point of no return,[2] beyond which you could not recover, the question is whether and how to "re-calibrate" the guidance, the wings and/or the zeal for Icarus to fly again or continue flying.

Whatever the reasons or the effects of de-internationalization, the question is whether the firm is willing and able to go back to the "game," to cross-border activities, to re-internationalize; how to re-internationalize to take advantage of new IB opportunities. Will it be a new or same guide, compass, passion, product or service, firm, path, gestalt, logic or BM? IB research has recently started addressing some of these re-internatio nalization-related questions.[3] However, compared to de-internationa lization, which has received a fair amount of attention (see Chap. 3), re-internationalization has yet to be studied systematically. Given the scarcity of research on re-internationalization, herein, we naturally raise more questions and inductively develop conjectures to guide research on re-internationalization, in general, and our quest in the book specifically, that is, how firms, following their de-internationalization, can re-internationalize with the help of BMI (Fig. 1.2).

4.2 Linking Re-internationalization to De-internationalization and Internationalization

The link between re-internationalization and de-internationalization is multifaceted. It goes without saying: a firm can re-internationalize only if it de-internationalized; similar to the link between de-internationalization and internationalization—de-internationalization could happen only if a firm internationalized first. These conjectures are depicted in Fig. 1.1 and exemplified in Vignette 4.1. The scope of re-internationalization could be defined by the de-internationalization typology (Fig. 3.2). A firm can re-internationalize following a total or partial withdrawal from its international activities (Quadrants I and II, respectively, in Fig. 3.2). A firm can re-internationalize after it ceases trading or right after it withdrew completely from its international activities (Quadrants IV, Fig. 3.2). This is a special case of re-internationalization when a firm resurrects like a phoenix from the ashes (Vignette 4.2).[4]

Vignette 4.1 De-internationalization and re-internationalization of General Motors
De-internationalizing

General Motors (GM) experienced significant turbulence during this period, where the firm initially expanded into global markets and acquired various brands worldwide,[5] but warning signs started to emerge in the late 1990s due to rising production costs, increased competition, and shifts in consumers preferences. Through the dawn of the new millennium, GM continued to experience financial challenges and followed a de-internationalization strategic shift to redraw and divest non-core brands and markets by refocusing its brand portfolio and strengthening and streamlining its operations.[6] In 2005, the firm closed several additional plants and reduced operations also in Europe and South Korea,[7] focusing instead on profitable markets (mostly in North America) with the Chevrolet and Cadillac core brands.

Cocooning

The global financial crisis of 2007–2008 did not spare GM, or the auto industry at large, either. The collapse of Lehmann Brothers triggered a chain reaction that led to stock markets collapsing, and large financial institutions and industrial firms went bankrupt or were bought up, millions of employees lost their jobs worldwide, and governments have had to come up with rescue packages to save their financial systems.[8] Faced with imminent collapse, GM had no choice but to file for Chapter 11 bankruptcy protection in June 2009,[9] which allowed the firm to restructure their business model.[10] In this phase, which we refer to as a "cocooning" phase, GM went through a massive restructuring, divesting unprofitable brands, closing numerous plants, and job cuts that reduced substantially operating expenses.[11] This "New GM" also focused on developing further "*…a leaner, faster and more customer-focused enterprise, consistent with the vision, goals and plans of GM's enhanced operating plan,*" [12] including promoting more funding for fuel-efficient and electric vehicles. Thus, the Cocooning phase was not just about cutting costs; it was also aimed towards a substantive, revised, strategic

(*continued*)

> **Vignette 4.1 (continued)**
> restructuring of the firm's business model as a whole. Including U.S. government partnership (receiving loans in exchange for significant ownership) and leadership change.[13]
>
> *Re-internationalizing*
> The cocooning phase was very brutal, but it paid off and achieved its primary goal, that is, not just to survive the crisis but also to thrive again. In doing so, GM followed a combination of retrenchment and strategic and brand re-positioning. In doing so, GM restructured and aligned with market trends. Investing in electrification R&D funds, directed toward hybrid and fully electric vehicle technology,[14] rebuilding its brand, and following a revised re-internationalization strategy who focused on emerging markets, particularly centered around China, being a crucial market in this automotive industry. Other strategic partnerships and alliances included re-internationalization efforts aimed toward India[15] and presence in South America, particularly through partnerships and subsidiaries in Brazil and Argentina.[16] Resilience and adaptability were key capabilities in this process. The revised strategy helped GM regain its competitive positioning and to brand itself again as one of the world's leading automotive manufacturers.[17]

The scope of re-internationalization could be further defined by the nature of de-internationalization. If de-internationalization is a failure (or perceived as a failure), then re-internationalization could be conceived as a correction of that failure, an *error-correction mechanism*. Saving face and firm reputation, gaining new support internally and externally, and capitalizing on new IB market opportunities could be achieved by re-internationalizing.

We further conjecture that the timing of correcting de-internationalization is pivotal to the success of re-internationalization. Two types of errors could be identified: *error of commission* (Re-e1), when a firm commits too early to re-internationalization, and *error of omission* (Re-e2), when a firm fails to take (full) advantage of a new IB market opportunity. Re-internationalizing too early (Re-e1) may escalate the failing course of action, deepening the de-internationalization of the firm, and likely leading to firm failure. By re-internationalizing late (Re-e2), a firm may loose on new market opportunities in the international markets.

We further assert that the link between re-internationalization and de-internationalization is indirectly dependent on internationalization. Internationalization can be a failure or perceived as a failure. It could be because of poor foreign market entry timing and velocity, misaligned configuration of firm resources and capabilities for the target market, wrong foreign market choice, and/or mismatch between the IB market opportunity and the firm BM, to name a few. In this instance, by de-internationalizing, a firm strives to correct that failure, internationalization.[18] If a firm de-internationalized earlier than required (De-e1 error of commission, see Chap. 3), then by re-internationalizing at or immediately after a partial or total withdrawal, the firm could be able to continue capitalizing on ongoing international market opportunities. If a firm de-internationalizes later than needed (De-e2 error of omission, see Chap. 3), then re-internationalization may have passed the real point of no return (Fig. 3.1) and becomes implausible as the likelihood of ceasing trading increases substantially. If the firm, assuming a false point of no return (Fig. 3.1), does pursue re-internationalization in this instance (Re-e1), it would further escalate its already ongoing commitment to a failing course of action and accelerate the demise of the firm.

If, as a result of ongoing internationalization and de-internationalization efforts, a firm totally withdraws from its international activities and ceases to exist at or immediately after its full de-internationalization (Quadrant IV, Fig. 3.2), the question is whether it is possible for this firm to re-internationalize. The evidence suggests, it is possible. Though as we mentioned earlier, this is a special, rare event—a phoenix-rising-from-the-ashes phenomenon (Vignette 4.2).

It follows that re-internationalization could be linked to de-internationalization in three ways:

Vignette 4.2 Phoenix-rising-from-the-ashes re-internationalization
Identifying and pursuing a market opportunity

The Case Firm (CF) is a software firm that produces estimation tools to predict costs and timescale of information technology projects customized for various managerial and engineering levels. CF was founded in 1992 (Fig. 4.1) by two entrepreneurs to sell software consulting services in the home market with the focus on object technology, client software, skills transfer, project mentoring, and training. Its main resource was human capital with ample experience in R&D and product-built-in know-how. Through their consulting services, by 1995, the founding entrepreneurs discovered a new market opportunity to develop a tangible product in the form of software. They discovered a problem project managers were facing—there was not an automated mechanism to measure the progress of a project, its expected effects, and impact. This led the firm to develop a software product. The first version of the product was launched in 1997 via an original equipment manufacturer deal (OEM) that was selling CF's product under own brand name. This deal was short-lived: it was terminated as soon as the OEM partner was acquired by a U.S. firm. CF managed to gain control of the product, re-brand it, and started own, direct sales in the home market (Fig. 4.1).

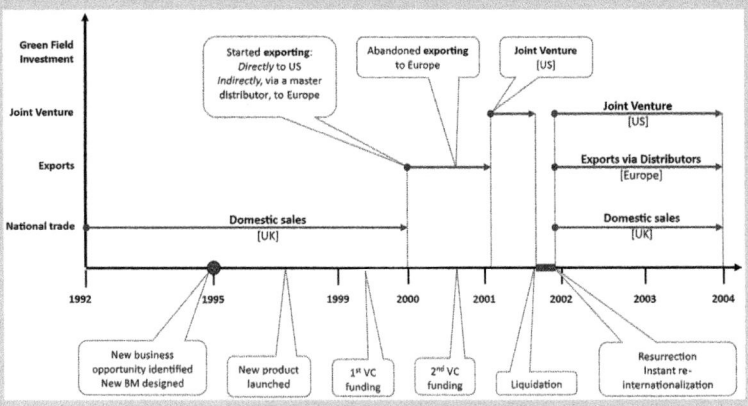

Fig. 4.1 From liquidation to resurrection to re-internationalization

(continued)

Vignette 4.2 (continued)
Internationalization

Establishing "*more of a real firm, with a unique selling point,*" as the CF CEO mentioned, demanded an investment BMI. The transition from service-led to product-led firm required new resources and capabilities, ways of organizing, dominant logic, growth path, and new BM. The founders wanted to start selling internationally. Following the development of U.K. market and acquisition of sufficient knowledge about and experience in selling the new product, CF envisaged a gradual internationalization pattern by entering a "psychically close" market, the U.S. market, via exporting a distributor. This approach, as per the CF founding team, would allow them to build and maintain good relationships with distributors. CF hired a non-executive with extensive background in selling and marketing software products worldwide. CF approached venture capitalists (VCs) to seek more resources, financial and expertise, to further pursue its internationalization plan for the United States. To receive the funding, CF had to modify its internationalization business plan as per VCs' request. VCs put a high priority on entering the U.S. and the EU market concurrently, and at a later stage—the global markets; the U.K. market was given a low priority. In the middle of 1999, CF received approximately £600,000, and a year later, £150,000.

De-internationalization

Series of internal and external factors led to CF de-internatio nalization. A tacit conflict had emerged between the founding team's and VCs' goals of internationalization pattern.[19] Although the founding entrepreneurs did not like VCs' internationalization, they agreed to and complied with it as the CF CEO mentioned: "*I do not think we could have taken a different route without major conflict. …At that time, both of us were completely new to this. And although, our gutfeel and instinct were telling us it was not right, it was very hard for us to justify. It was incredibly frustrated, stressful. It gives you a sense that you've lost control of something that you used to view as yours.*" This resulted in CF focusing on U.S. and U.K. markets

(*continued*)

Vignette 4.2 (continued)
and putting "tacitly" the EU market "*on the backburner*," as a co-founder mentioned. In 2000, the IT market in the United States started to collapse, affecting gradually the EU market and the rest of the world, with lots of IT firms disappearing.[20] CF sales from international activity dropped from 30% in 1999 to 0% in 2000.

Resurrection

At the end of 2000, VCs brought in own non-executive with expertise in crisis management. In the early of 2001, CF signed a joint-venture agreement with a UK-based software tools firm that had a strong customer base in the United States in an attempt to maintain its (ad)venture in the United States. Another revival plan that CF presented to VCs was to "*cocoon*" to get through that tough period. Plan C, should the other two not work, was a "liquidation scenario," and the new non-executive introduced CF to a liquidator. Neither the US-market-maintenance plan nor the cocoon plan was accepted by the investors, and as a result the founders made a decision to voluntarily liquidate the firm. CF was liquidated in September of 2001 (corresponding to Quadrant IV: total withdrawal from international activities and ceased trading immediately," Fig. 3.2). By the end of November, the founders "resurrected" the firm by buying-back the IP from the liquidator and re-hiring the senior software engineer.

Re-internationalization

The minimum safety net or withstanding gestalt (Fig. 3.1) that allowed CF to re-internationalize consisted of the founding entrepreneurs, the IP, senior engineer, and the key account (the joint-venture partner). Following the purchase of the IP from the liquidator, CF re-branded the software and launched its first release in December of 2001. Having retained a strong relationship with its joint-venture partner, CF re-internationalized following the launch of the newly branded product. A testimony of its success that followed is a sales deal CF signed in 2004 with a large U.S. defense firm. By 2005, according to an American software magazine, CF was one of the leaders in the project software market.

(1) If de-internationalization is a failure or perceived as a failure, then re-internationalization would be an error-correcting mechanism (Re-e1, Re-e2) that could:

   a. deepen de-internationalization, escalate the failing course of the firm, leading to the firm end; or
   b. prevent the firm from taking advantage of new international market opportunities.

(2) If de-internationalization corrects (De-e1, De-e2) a failing internationalization, then re-internationalization could:

   a. help the firm to take advantage of the extant international market opportunities by reversing fully or partly firm withdrawal, thus mitigating the risks of failure; or
   b. escalate an ongoing commitment to a failing course of action, accelerating the demise of the firm; and

(3) If de-internationalization leads to the closure of the firm, then re-internationalization in the form of a phoenix-rising-from-the-ashes could revive the firm.

"Being reactive" is a joint property of these links. They are designed to react to a state of de-internationalization. There might be another type of link between re-internationalization and de-internationalization—an entrepreneurial link. Rather than reacting to a state of de-internationalization, re-internationalization could be employed by a firm as an entrepreneurial activity whereby it proactively seeks new international market opportunities and proactively pursues these opportunities by redesigning its BM or designing a new one.

4.3 Defining Re-internationalization

Conceptualization of the links between re-internationalization, de-internationalization, and internationalization is a step toward defining re-internationalization, but not, in itself, sufficient. To arrive at a definition of re-internationalization, it is pivotal next to underscore the positioning of re-internationalization in the cross-border activity of a firm and highlight key concepts, elements, and properties of re-internationalization. One of the main themes of this book is a holistic perspective of the cross-border of the firm that views *"internationalization, de-internationalization,* and *re-internationalization*" as part of the "*cross-border activity*" of the firm.[21] The discussion above of the links between these three types is within this holistic view of cross-border activity. Within the same perspective, cross-border activity is viewed as an *organizational gestalt* that consists of *mutually supportive capacity, pattern, and dominant logic*. This conceptualization of a cross-border activity of a firm suggests that each cross-border activity type has its own pattern, capacity, and logic.

Re-internationalization thus has its own pattern, capacity, and logic that supports re-internationalization of the firm. This points to the *duality* of re-internationalization defined as a *process* (re-internationalization pattern) and a *state* (re-internationalization capacity). Firms may re-internationalize *gradually*, after a "time-out" following de-internationalization, or *instantly* immediately after de-internationalization. In addition to these two types of "velocity," "timing" is another key factor for re-internationalization. Within either of these two velocities, a firm may commit too early (error of commission, Re-e1) or too late (error of omission, Re-e2) to re-internationalization.

A commitment of the firm to re-internationalize implies a reconfiguration of its pattern, capacity, and logic. Following a total withdrawal from international activities (Quadrant I, Fig. 3.2), a firm could re-internationalize by employing the same approach to pattern, capacity, and logic configuration as in its first-time internationalization. Compared to first-time internationalization, re-internationalization will be moderated by newly acquired or lost experience, resources, and capabilities—positive or negative—from internationalization and de-internationalization. If, for example, a first-time internationalization pattern, capacity, or logic configuration turns out to be a failure and totally de-internationalize as a result, a firm will face a series of concerns: how much was learned; is this learning useful; how much to unlearn; can it be unlearned; if yes, how; target same market(s) or new one(s); become risk averse or risk taker; go back to "the game" immediately or take a "time-off." Whether first-time internationalization is a success or failure, re-internationalization, following a total withdrawal from international activities, will benefit from comparing it to and contrasting it with first-time internationalization by zooming in and zooming out within and across respective configurations of patterns, capacities, and logics (see Chap. 5).

Re-internationalization following a partial withdrawal from international activities (Quadrant II and Quadrant IV, Fig. 3.2; see also Vignette 4.2) is more complex. A firm can re-internationalize by opening an R&D

facility in a psychically distant market following the closure of a sales office located in a nearby, physically close market. Or a firm can re-internationalize by acquiring a local firm following a period of direct exporting in that market that was a result of de-franchising, which was the initial entry mode of its first-time internationalization. The complexity of re-internationalization increases by adding the outcomes of internationalization and de-internationalization, their successes, or failures, or the mix of entry modes and target countries (mode-country packages). Reconfiguring a re-internationalization gestalt—pattern, capacity, and logic—for the purpose of continual cross-border activities is daunting. Concurrent or consecutive zooming in on and out of these diverse re-internationalization patterns, capacities, and logics will contribute to a successful reconfiguration of re-internationalization gestalt(s).

Following this discussion, we define re-internationalization as *a process and a state that allows a firm to re-configure its pattern, capacity, and logic to gradually or instantly cross national borders following total or partial de-internationalization.* "Pattern" captures *how, why, when what, where, who, and with whom* of re-internationalization. "Capacity" encapsulates, inter alia, resources, capabilities, processes, structures, strategies, experiences, and motivations to re-internationalize. "Gradual or instant" defines re-internationalization "velocity." "Partial or total de-internationalization" points to a direct link between re-internationalization and de-internationalization and an indirect link between re-internationalization and internationalization that is mediated by de-internationalization.

4.4 The "whys" of Re-internationalization

As with internationalization, *external* and *internal* stimuli drive re-internationalization.[22] External stimuli could be new foreign market opportunities; attractive tariffs, product regulation, FDI incentives; favorable currency movement; unsolicited orders; new network partner; saturated domestic or foreign market; or increased competition in the home or foreign market. Internal stimuli could be entrepreneurial, managerial urge, or motivation; economies of scale or scope; unique product or technology and other firm-specific advantages; risk mitigation and diversification; available production capacity at home or abroad; or diminishing sales in the domestic and/or foreign market. It can be noticed that firms, triggered by these stimuli, can be *proactive* or *reactive* in their pursuit of re-internationalization. For example, identifying and pursuing a new international market opportunity or taking advantage of a unique product or technology are proactive approaches to re-internationalization. Following or joining a new partner internationally or mitigating and/or diversifying the risks within or across mode-country packages points toward a reactive approach to re-internationalization.

Internationalization and de-internationalization experiences also play important roles in deciding whether to re-internationalize or not. It might be stating the obvious, but nonetheless, it is pivotal to underscore here that a firm that re-internationalizes is not the same as it was when it de-internationalized or internationalized. Re-internationalization is shaped by these experiences, by the ability of the firm to learn and unlearn in the aftermath of de-internationalization. The nature and degree of these experiences, associated knowledge acquisition, learning, and unlearning further impact the re-internationalization of the firm.[23]

They can be positive or negative with marginal or substantial impact on the firm. For example, internationalization or de-internationalization can be a failure, leading to a total withdrawal from cross-border activities, downsizing as a result of the firm to its withstanding gestalt (see Chap. 3), followed by instant re-internationalization to the same foreign market following the same internationalization footprint (Re-e1, error of commission), thus increasing the likelihood of failure. This mini case also highlights the importance and the impact of the entrepreneurial or managerial urge, motivation, and perceptions toward the need to re-internationalize. It also hints at decision-makers' re-internationalization orientation posture, e.g., have they become more or less risk averse, more or less proactive, or more or less able to learn and unlearn? The next main concern is *how* to translate internal and external stimuli and experiences from internationalization and de-internationalization into opportunities for re-internationalization.

4.5 The "hows" of Re-internationalization

The conceptualization of the "hows" of re-internationalization is based on a series of factors. It is based on the *cyclical* nature of cross-border activities of firms (Fig. 1.1). It is also founded on our conjecture that re-internationalization *directly* depends on de-internationalization and *indirectly* on internationalization, being *mediated* by de-internationalization. Another assumption that this conceptualization is founded on is the nature of triggering events in this cyclical process of cross-border activity of the firm, namely, *critical events*. These are events that deviate negatively or positively from what is normal or expected.

A critical event may render the internationalization of the firm unfeasible (e.g., a firm withdraws from its international activities being made redundant following a restructuring of a MNE value chain), unprofitable (e.g., a firm realizes that internationalization was a mistake and decides to de-internationalize), or unattractive (e.g., a firm withdraws from its international activity having identified a new international market opportunity with bigger potential returns and lesser risks).

When considering timing and velocity of de-internationalization, firms must factor in their real point-of-no return to avoid being trapped into pursuing a false point-of-no return (Fig. 3.1); errors of de-internationalization: De-e1, error of commission and De-e2, error of omission; and types of withdrawal, total and/or partial (Fig. 3.2). Critical events such as "wait-and-see" (e.g., maybe it will turn profitable); attempt to salvage sunk costs (e.g., redundant, so what? Let's find another value chain partner); high closing, exit costs; and job security threat (e.g., let's make this attractive otherwise we are gone) may lead to a late withdrawal (De-e2), increasing the risk of failure, especially if the real point-of-no return is passed. "Jumping on the bandwagon" to pursue a new international market opportunity, "installation" of new management, and overconfidence in the ability to learn and unlearn could make the firm "pull the plug" too early (De-e1). This would reduce (maybe substantially) possible gains from ongoing opportunities in the international markets, but, in turn, will decrease the likelihood of failure following de-internatio nalization.

The above suggests that "how" a firm re-internationalizes depends on the success and failure of its de-internationalization and internationalization (Fig. 4.2). When de-internationalization is successful following a successful internationalization (Quadrant I), a firm may re-internationalize by *imitating partially or totally* its internationalization gestalt: pattern, capacity, and logic. When de-internationalization is successful following an unsuccessful internationalization (Quadrant II), a firm may re-internationalize by designing a new internationalization gestalt, previously unknown to or untried by the firm. Here we conjecture that the likelihood of miscalculating the real point-of-no-return is high when a De-e2 error (error of omission) is made and, thus, increases the likelihood of failure. When de-internationalization is unsuccessful following an unsuccessful internationalization (Quadrant III), a firm can re-internationalize only after taking "time-off" period to rethink and innovate not only its internationalization gestalt but also the entire gestalt of the firm, which will be

	Internationalization	
	Successful	Unsuccessful
De-internationalization — Successful	**I** **Imitating** (Imitate partially or totally internationalization gestalt)	**II** **Rejuvenating** (Design a new internationalization gestalt)
De-internationalization — Unsuccessful	**IV** **Balancing** (Partial or total imitation of <u>or</u> design a new internationalization gestalt)	**III** **Taking 'time-off'** (Design a new organizational gestalt)

Fig. 4.2 The typology of re-internationalization

redesigned. When de-internationalization is unsuccessful following a successful internationalization (Quadrant IV), a firm can re-internationalize either by imitating partially or totally its internationalization gestalt (e.g., having been made redundant, the firm makes a De-e2 error (error of omission) but manages to eventually withdraw and re-internationalize) or by designing a completely new internationalization gestalt (e.g., if existing internationalization gestalt is no longer attractive, but the new international market opportunity demands a new internationalization pattern, capacity, and logic). In each of these quadrants, the firm commitment to a re-internationalization mode or mode-package, risks and costs of an entry mode or mode-package (see Chap. 2) will moderate the configuration of the firm re-internationalization gestalt: pattern, capacity, and logic.

4.6 Concluding Remarks

When compared to the other two types of cross-border activity, internationalization and de-internationalization, re-internationalization is the least researched and understood. Anecdotal evidence suggests it *is* practiced, but it has yet to be studied systematically. This led us to develop an inductively conceptual and theoretical understanding of re-internationalization. Building on its relationship with and dependence on de-internationalization (directly) and internationalization (indirectly), we defined re-internationalization; proposed two *outcomes* of re-internationalization, *total* and *partial*; posited two *errors* of re-internationalization, error of *commission* (Re-e1) and error of *omission* (Re-e2); and developed a *typology* of re-internationalization and its four types: *imitating, balancing, rejuvenating*, and *taking time-off*. All these new theoretical advancements will facilitate research of re-internationalization within and outside IB to enable the understanding and practice of re-internationalization.

Notes

1. Ovid (1955, p. 184).
2. Turcan (2006, 2013).
3. Aguzzoli et al. (2021), Ali and Mathur (2022), Freeman et al. (2013), Kafouros et al. (2022), Surdu and Narula (2021), Vissak and Francioni (2013), Welch and Welch (2009), Yu et al. (2022).
4. Adapted from Turcan (2006).
5. L.A. Times (2000).
6. Isaacs (2006).
7. BBC (2004).
8. Taran et al. (2022).
9. The Guardian (2009).
10. US Treasury (2009).
11. Goldman and Valdes-Dapena (2009), Goldstein (2009), Smith (2009).
12. General Motors Corporation (2009).
13. Vlasic (2009).
14. GM electrification vision "Our Path to an All-Electric Future: Zero Crashes, Zero Emissions, Zero Congestion" (GM, 2024).
15. The Associated Press (2007).
16. GM Brazil (2024), GM Argentina (2024).
17. DeBord (2018).
18. Turcan (2006).
19. Turcan (2008).
20. This was amid the dot.com bubble that picked and burst in 2000.
21. Turcan (2003, 2006).
22. Aguzzoli et al. (2021), Javalgi et al. (2011), Kafouros et al. (2022).
23. Ali and Mathur (2022), da Fonseca and da Rocha (2023), Ganotakis et al. (2022), Javalgi et al. (2011), Kafouros et al. (2022), Surdu and Narula (2021), Yu et al. (2022).

REFERENCES

Aguzzoli, R., Lengler, J., Sousa, C. M., & Benito, G. R. (2021). Here we go again: A case study on re-entering a foreign market. *British Journal of Management, 32*(2), 416–434.

Ali, S., & Mathur, A. N. (2022). When failure is neither fatal nor final: Understanding re-internationalization processes. *American Business Review, 25*(1), 5.

Associated Press. (2007). GM thinks small in India, reaps big reward. *NBC News*. https://t.ly/oTJ5z

BBC News. (2004). GM to cut 12,000 jobs in Europe. *BBC News*. https://t.ly/VAlSn

da Fonseca, L. N. M., & da Rocha, A. (2023). Setbacks, interruptions and turnarounds in the internationalization process: A bibliometric and literature review of de-internationalization. *Management Review Quarterly, 73*(3), 1351–1384.

DeBord, M. (2018, October 20). How GM went from a government bailout and bankruptcy to being one of the world's best-run car companies a decade later. *Business Insider*. https://t.ly/1hm3p

Freeman, S., Deligonul, S., & Cavusgil, T. (2013). Strategic re-structuring by born-globals using outward and inward-oriented activity. *International Marketing Review, 30*(2), 156–182.

Ganotakis, P., Konara, P., Kafouros, M., & Love, J. H. (2022). Taking a time-out from exporting: Implications for the likelihood of export re-entry and re-entry export performance. *Journal of World Business, 57*(5), 101349.

General Motors Corporation. (2009). GM announced agreement with U.S. Treasury and Canadian governments providing fast track to competitive future for "New GM." Retrieved April 18, 2024, from https://t.ly/ag5RM

GM. (2024). Our path to an all-electric future: Zero crashes, zero emissions, zero congestion. Retrieved April 18, 2024, from https://t.ly/bRBq0

GM Argentina. (2024). GM de Argentina. Retrieved April 18, 2024, from https://t.ly/GWcSd

GM Brazil. (2024). GM website-global presence: Brazil. Retrieved April 18, 2024, from https://t.ly/ke6R7

Goldman, D., & Valdes-Dapena, P. (2009). GM to sell Saturn to Penske. *CNN Money*. Retrieved April 18, 2024 from https://t.ly/v7e7t

Goldstein, S. (2009, June 16). GM, Koenigsegg reach tentative Saab deal. *MarketWatch*. https://t.ly/m4yxj

Isaacs, D. (2006). General Motors lost $8.6 billion in 2005. *World Socialist Web Site*. Retrieved April 18, 2024, from https://t.ly/F_vVu

Javalgi, R. G., Deligonul, S., Dixit, A., & Cavusgil, S. T. (2011). International market reentry: A review and research framework. *International Business Review, 20*(4), 377–393.

Kafouros, M., Cavusgil, S. T., Devinney, T. M., Ganotakis, P., & Fainshmidt, S. (2022). Cycles of de-internationalization and re-internationalization: Towards an integrative framework. *Journal of World Business, 57*(1), 101257.
L.A. Times. (2000). Retrieved April 18th, 2024 from https://t.ly/PSILC
Ovid. (1955). *Metamorphoses* (p. 184). Penguin Classics.
Smith, A. (2009, June 2). GM unloads Hummer to Chinese buyer. *CNN Money.* https://t.ly/yPNxy
Surdu, I., & Narula, R. (2021). Organizational learning, unlearning and re-internationalization timing: Differences between emerging- versus developed-market MNEs. *Journal of International Management, 27*(3), 100784.
Taran, Y., Boer, H., & Nielsen, C. (2022). *The business model innovation process: Preparation, organization and management.* Routledge.
The Guardian. (2009). Retrieved April 18th, 2024 from https://t.ly/UuCTp
Turcan, R. V. (2003). De-internationalization and the small firm. In C. Wheeler, F. McDonald, & I. Greaves (Eds.), *Internationalization: Firms strategies and management* (pp. 208–222). Palgrave.
Turcan, R. V. (2006). De-internationalization of small high-technology firms: An international entrepreneurship perspective. Doctoral dissertation, University of Strathclyde, Glasgow, UK.
Ţurcan, R. V. (2008). Entrepreneur–venture capitalist relationships: Mitigating post-investment dyadic tensions. *Venture Capital, 10*(3), 281–304.
Turcan, R. V. (2013). The philosophy of turning points: A case of de-internationalization. *Advances in International Management, 26,* 219–235.
U.S. Dept. of the Treasury. (2009). General Motors Corporation 2009–2014 restructuring plan. Retrieved April 15, 2024, from https://t.ly/3P9yW
Vissak, T., & Francioni, B. (2013). Serial nonlinear internationalization in practice: A case study. *International Business Review, 22*(6), 951–962.
Vlasic, B. (2009, December 2). G.M. asked its chief to resign. *The New York Times.* https://t.ly/nJ7ez
Welch, C. L., & Welch, L. S. (2009). Re-internationalization: Exploration and conceptualisation. *International Business Review, 18*(6), 567–577.
Yu, H., Fletcher, M., & Buck, T. (2022). Managing digital transformation during re-internationalization: Trajectories and implications for performance. *Journal of International Management, 28*(4), 100947.

CHAPTER 5

Business Model Innovation

If you have genius, industry will improve it; if you have none, industry will supply its place.
—Sir Joshua Reynolds

5.1 Weathering the Storm

In "calm waters," why bother changing anything? As the saying goes, "if it ain't broke, don't fix it."[1] But wasn't the "frog boiled," because it got too comfortable, unable to see the "storm" coming? When a "course" is set, whether by a new or well-established firm, it follows its dominant logic, an adopted business model, a critical resource allocation design. The dominant logic not only delineates the "status quo" of the firm[2] but also contributes to its competitiveness.[3] It is also what contributes to the growth and success of the firm, to its revenue and profits.

A firm adopting a dominant organizational gestalt can get "too comfortable" and find itself trapped in or blinded by it (as we discussed in previous chapters). Entrapment or blindness can prevent the firm from seeing the threats or new opportunities. It can discourage the firm from changing its business model, its "sailing" course from internationalization to de-internationalization and re-internationalization. To mitigate the

© The Author(s), under exclusive license to Springer Nature Switzerland AG 2025
J. C. Sort et al., *De-internationalization and Re-internationalization of the Firm*,
https://doi.org/10.1007/978-3-031-81774-8_5

risks of entrapment or blindness, the firm can engage in BMI as a source of superior performance for new and established firms (Fig. 1.2).[4] We define BMI as "*a process of reconfiguring organizational gestalt (pattern, capacity and logic)*." Whether in calm or stormy waters, the firms can experiment, inter alia, with BMI types and BM configurations to reconfigure their organizational gestalts to avoid traps and open the blinders. These are unfolded in this chapter.

5.2 Defining BMI

5.2.1 BMI Types

BMI types contribute to the design of new BMs and/or reconfiguration of existing BMs.[5] BMI can be conceptualized as models (vehicles) of change, e.g., *realization model* (main concern is how to exploit the current potential within an existing operational framework); *renewal model* (main concern is how to create a new position on the price/value curve); *extension model* (main concern is new markets, value chain functions, and product/service lines development through radical changes); and *journey model* (main concern is how to realize a complete transformation of the original BM.[6]

At the radical end of the innovation spectrum,[7] there could be identified three BMI types: *enterprise model innovation*, with a focus on "specializing and reconfiguring the business to deliver greater value by rethinking what is done in-house and through collaboration;" *industry model innovation*, with a focus on "redefining an existing industry, moving into a new industry, or creating an entirely new one;" and *revenue model innovation*, with a focus on "changing how revenue is generated through new value propositions and new pricing models."[8]

To explore the innovation of de-internationalization and re-internationalization, we employ the following four BMI types and related sub-types[9] (see also Vignette 5.1):

Vignette 5.1 Open innovation at LEGO
LEGO Group, a leading Danish construction toy production firm based in Billund, Denmark, leveraged multiple open innovation strategies. It launched an online platform for fans, LEGO Ideas,[10] where users can submit their ideas and vote on their favorite ones. This *inbound outside-in open innovation* approach can help LEGO to get closer to its fans and users and harness (also) external community collective creativity. Thus, part of the product innovation ideation and selection process is now initiated through a democratized[11] platform with users and fans.

An example of an *inside-out open innovation* strategy is represented in LEGO's Serious Play,[12] where the new target customers are adults, not children. This facilitated workshop method, using LEGO bricks, enabled the new users to deal with complex problems in a creative manner, where participants can exhibit metaphorical[13] models that represent their thoughts and perspective viewpoints. Through these workshops, LEGO leverages the collective intelligence[14] of leaders and staff to introduce new possible novel solutions.

LEGO also followed an *outside-in* and *inside-out open innovation* strategy by establishing new partnerships with various entertainment firms, like Warner Bros.[15] and Disney,[16] and developed themes based on popular franchises. For example, the Warner Bros. collaboration produced iconic franchises like DC Comics, including *Batman*, *Superman*, *Harry Potter*, *The Lord of the Rings*,[17] and *Scooby-Doo*.[18] Most involved *outside-in licensing* agreements that allowed LEGO to tap into external intellectual properties and access to entirely new offering lines and audiences, expanding their market reach. This collaboration agreement did not stop in the manufacturing of physical items but continued at the introduction of new video games and animated-related content offerings.[19] Similarly, LEGO followed such licensed partnership with Disney, a longstanding partner, by producing sets based on popular franchises such as *Marvel Superheroes* and *Star Wars*. Other instances of partnership and co-branding agreements include IKEA, NIKE, MoMA (Museum of Modern Art), Adidas, Levi's, to name a few.[20]

(continued)

Vignette 5.1 (continued)

Another partnership worth mentioning that followed an *inside-out and an outside* in collaborative innovation is with NASA, where LEGO leveraged its internal resources, expertise, and brand identity, as well as NASA's resources and scientists, to co-create space exploration experiences offerings.[21] An additional collaborative innovation with NASA included educational programs that aimed to inspire interest with STEM education among children through space explorations. In collaboration with NASA's STEM Engagement Office,[22] various classroom activities, robotics challenges, and curriculum supplements were developed, inspired by NASA's missions and discoveries.[23]

Another *inside-out* strategic path adopted by LEGO is LEGOLAND Parks,[24] which involve a joint venture with other firms (e.g., Merlin Entertainments)[25] that are specialized in theme park development and management. It is worth mentioning that *LEGO Ventures*,[26] (*outside-out*) venture capital arm of the LEGO group, invested in various startup firms and entrepreneurs who focus on developing new offering experiences related to play, learning, and creativity.

By continuously forging new strategic partnerships, LEGO's open innovation journey fostered its continuous innovation culture and maintained its leading role in its industry, with a positive spillover to other industries, while maintaining its strong brand loyalty and its thriving business.

1. *(Semi) Closed* BMI:
    1.1 *Closed, inside-in BMI*: Internal competences are used to innovate the existing core business.
    1.2 *Open, outside-in BMI*: External ideas and competences are used to innovate the existing core business through, for example, a merger, an acquisition, or licensing in another firm's IPR.
2. *Open BMI:*
    2.1 *Open, inside-out BMI*: Internal competences are used to create a new business model spun off from the existing organization in a separate business unit or division.

2.2 *Open, inside-out/outside-in BMI*: A strategic alliance or joint venture is established with another firm to develop and implement a new BM. In both cases, an additional BM is developed, typically organized in the form of another business unit or division, or as a strategic alliance or a joint venture together with another firm.
3. *From scratch BMI*:
   3.1 *Spin-offs firms*, started by one or two firm employees, who decide to leave their jobs and start up their own business: a hairdresser, a flower shop, a small capability-based job shop supplying parts and components to several assembly firms. One of the most famous examples in this category is Intel. Examples may also include small high-tech firms as university spin-offs.
   3.2 *"Garage" firms*: Many of these firms remain small, but some develop into highly innovative, dominant design breakers, reach the popular press, and are household names today. Examples include Hewlett-Packard, Microsoft, Apple, Amazon, and Google.
4. *Network-level BMI*: Many firms are finding themselves increasingly "tied" to other firms, adjusting own BMs to support their partners' core competences by joining existing or creating new platforms for collaboration and innovation. In this instance, it is the platform that is considered as the unit of analysis, e.g., joint synergies and network-level operations.

5.2.2 Zooming-in and Zooming-out

BMI can occur during the production activities of the firm (e.g., designing, purchasing, and manufacturing), and its sales activities (e.g., finding and reaching customers, selling and distributing products/services).[27] It can take place also beyond the value chain, at the exchange and transaction mechanisms and process of the firm.[28] The innovation can happen at the structure and network of the firm, e.g., alliances, joint ventures, outsourcing, licensing, and spin-offs.[29] This multi-level view on innovation suggests not only that the business model is more than the mere sum of its individual parts[30] but that, as a unit of analysis for innovation, the business model has a wider scope than the firm boundaries, since it may encompass the capabilities of multiple firms in multiple industries. It also suggests that a systemic view of the business model and its innovation is warranted. Such a systemic view lies at the heart of BMI. It is founded on combining and amplifying—*zooming-in* and *zooming-out*[31]—individual and collective parts of business models across various levels of operation, micro, meso, and macro (see Vignette 5.2) to allow decision-makers to develop a nuanced (by zooming in) and/or holistic understanding (by zooming out) of what, how, and when to innovate.

> **Vignette 5.2 Zooming-in and zooming-out at Alpha**
> Alpha decides to expand its operations into a new international market. This decision requires a thorough development of its internationalization gestalt (internationalization pattern, capacity, and logic) and related business model. The iteration between zooming-in and zooming-out and abstracting can contribute to this process.
>
> *Abstracting:* while planning for internationalization, the firm focuses, inter alia, on understanding its market dynamics, customer preferences, and competitive landscape. In doing so, it seeks to identify potential countries for expansion, barriers and regulations in the designated country, and possible market entry strategies (e.g., joint venture, exporting, or local subsidiary). The entry strategy would depend, for example, on foreign market regulatory compliance and potential changes needed in the firm's global supply chain management. From a BM configuration perspective, adapting its BM to suit the new market profile requires to leverage currently established, or potentially new, BM configurations. To achieve this, decision-makers must abstract toward the first-level of abstraction, BM configurations, to examine potential BM configurations to support the market entry. These could be, for example, a basic freemium model with advanced features through paid subscription; a multi-sided platform, where the firm serves as an intermediary; a subscription model; or a direct sales model.
>
> *Zooming-in:* From a value chain perspective, the firm needs to assess, for example, its operations, inbound and outbound logistics. This will also have implications on manufacturing, delivery, and customer service to fit the new market needs, considering local suppliers and distribution networks. Wishing to establish local manufacturing, Alpha would zoom-in on the "Value configuration" driver to discover several sub-model configurations to pursue:
>
> (*continued*)

> **Vignette 5.2 (continued)**
>
> - TQM (Total Quality Management)—ensuring product quality that meets international standards.
> - JIT (Just in Time)—to reduce waste and improve efficiency.
> - Kanban—for effective production scheduling.
> - Inventory management—to secure optimal inventory levels and production flow, based on expected local demand.
> - Job design—design job roles that ensure efficiency and compliance.
>
> *Zooming-out:* That information can be brought back to the level of the value chain of the firm to understand challenges and actions to be taken related to, for example, firm performance. The decisions made at this value configuration level will have implications on other value drivers. For example, new local partner network, operational and logistics costs management, and adjustments to new revenue streams (e.g., product sales; service revenues; commission fees). These changes, eventually, will be further integrated and aligned with the overall cross-border activity of the firm.

Zooming-in is a micro-level focus on operating business processes to "break down" these processes into their individual components or value drivers, delving deeper into specific elements and sub-models, and subsequently ascending to a higher level of abstraction "armed" with detailed insights about these processes.[32] Zooming-in is largely confined to the boundaries of the firm.

Zooming-out from the operating business processes takes a meso- or macro-level perspective on external factors affecting the current operating BM. It entails, inter alia, examining and understanding the ecosystem in which the firm operates, including its key stakeholders, the competitive landscape, industry trends, institutional logics, technological advances, and societal changes. Zooming-out helps decision-makers, for example, align the dominant logic of the firm with identified opportunities and threats and gain insights into the strategic positioning and the firm's potential growth (including cross-border) trajectory.

Iterating between zooming-in and zooming-out allows decision-makers not only to view the entire business, a bigger picture (helicopter view), but also a detailed relation within and between components of the system by breaking it down into partial sub-models and delving deeper into specific BM elements.[33] In other words, to understand how to innovate a business model, there is a need to break it down into individual components, and understand how their complementary, value-creating properties fit together in a holistic way to ensure a cumulative effect.[34]

Abstracting can help decision-makers in their BMI efforts during the iteration between zooming-in and zooming-out. It is about conceptualizing a BM of a firm at a higher level of abstraction via diverse modes and levels of abstraction. For example, decision-makers can abstract[35] from the operational level to the highest level of abstraction, BM *narratives* or to the first level of abstraction, BM *configurations* (or meta-models).[36]

The iteration between zooming-in and zooming-out and abstracting via diverse levels and modes of abstraction can shed light not only on the current, operational processes and strategy of the firm but also on new ways of organizing and new value-creation opportunities.[37] It can aid practitioners develop a nuanced and holistic understanding of BM, gain a deeper understanding of the complex dynamics at play, and provide valuable BMI insights.

5.3 BM Configurations and the 5-V Framework

BM configurations[38] are BM "formulae" that have been tried and tested in other firms, industries, or markets.[39] They enable decision-makers, inter alia, to get out of entrapment and open the blinds to innovate their firms' BMs (Vignette 5.3). It is important to note that BM configurations[40] should not be viewed as an exhaustive list of possible BMI "receipts" as new BM configurations continuously emerge. In our book, we build on the 5-V framework that categorizes 71 BM configurations into Five Value Drivers:[41]

- *Value proposition* is a firm's offer of products and services that satisfy customer needs for which customers are willing to pay.[42] An example of such a value proposition is "no frills," where a firm attempts to offer a lower price or service than traditional offerings, for example, Ryanair.
- *Value segment* is a customer segment (or segments) a firm aims to serve and how the firm intends to establish relationships with customers.[43] "Round up buyers" exemplify this value, where buyers are

> **Vignette 5.3 5-V framework at Spotify**
> With its innovative streaming platform, Spotify succeeded in transforming the music industry.[47] Entered the market in 2006 when the music industry was saturated with piracy, and users were eager to find new and legal ways to download music for free, the firm demonstrated how an effective combination mix of various business model configurations can generate a powerful and sustained operating business model and to position themselves as a leader in the music industry, and later on also in the podcasting space. Here's how they achieved this:
>
> - *Value Proposition*: "Mass-customized commodity"[48]—customized model options (i.e., have it your way) along with competitive prices and fast delivery.
> - *Value Segment*: "Multi-sided platforms"[49]—create value by facilitating interactions between two or more distinct but interdependent groups of customers, that is, content creators (musicians and podcasters) on one side and users on the other.
> - *Value Configurations*: "Disintermediation"[50] by delivering its offerings directly to the customer, rather than through intermediary channels.
> - *Value Network*: a possible mix of two configurations: "Adaptive"[51]—creating an ecosystem by establishing its technologies as the basis for a platform of innovation for the value chain and benefit from the investments of others on the platform; and "Outside-in"[52] by gathering values and information from external parties.
> - *Value Capture*: a "Freemium"[53] model, where a free ad-supported option is available for users alongside a variety of premium subscription options.

"rounded up" to gain purchase discounts and attractive prices; Costco offers an example of this segment.
- *Value configuration* is a mix of key resources that enable a firm's key activities that create, produce, and deliver the value proposition effectively to the target value segments[44] and the cost structure needed to make the business model work. An external sales force is an example of this when a firm uses direct sales through an external sales force to enhance its sales, which can be observed in, for example, Tupperware and Vorwerk.

- *Value network* is a network of partners who engage in different types of cooperation with the firm to achieve economies of scale or scope, risk reduction, or to tap into new knowledge or resources.[45] Franchising is a case where the owner licenses the product or service to a dealer (franchisee). McDonald's and Starbucks offer such examples.
- *Value Capture* is about how and how much the customers pay for the delivered products or services.[46] Freemium illustrates value capture, in which customers are offered the basic offering for free but pay for more features. Such freemium value captures are found in, for example, Skype, LinkedIn, and YouTube.

5.4 Concluding Remarks

A consensus has emerged among academics and practitioners that BMI matters.[54] BMI helps decision-makers reconfigure organizational gestalts of their firms. It can take place within cross-border activity gestalts: internationalization, de-internationalization, and re-internationalization. Within each, decision-makers can adopt a mix of BMI strategies to develop respective business models to support an organizational gestalt. BMI strategies are abstracting, zooming-in, zooming-out, and iterating. Abstracting helps decision-makers conceptualize their firms away from "the real" firm or reality to a higher level of abstraction. Zooming-in and zooming-out and the iteration between the two allow decision-makers to combine and amplify individual and collective parts of business models across various levels of operation, micro, meso, and macro. To explore the intersection of de-internationalization and re-internationalization (which is the focus of the next two chapters), we employ the BMI configuration framework, which is the first level of abstraction and BMI types.

Notes

1. Bert Lance.
2. Magretta (2002).
3. Casadesus-Masanell and Ricart (2010).
4. Chesbrough and Rosenbloom (2002), Taran et al. (2022).
5. Massa and Tucci (2013), Taran et al. (2022). For example, Toyota, IBM, and Kodak innovated their existing BMs. Nespresso is an example of a new BM created by Nestlé in addition to and separated from its existing busi-

ness. Apple, Microsoft, Ryanair, and Amazon are examples of new BMs supporting entirely new venues.
6. Linder and Cantrell (2000).
7. The debate on incremental versus radical innovation (e.g., Leifer, 2002; Rosenstand et al., 2023; Tidd & Bessant, 2009) centers on these two main questions: "how new" and "new to whom".
8. IBM (2010, p. 29). IBM reported in 2006 that the business model innovators they surveyed outperformed their competitors in operating margin growth by 5% over five years, while product, service, market, and process innovators witnessed virtually no growth. Note: business model innovations, especially the more radical ones, are much rarer than product, service, and process innovation. IBM encourages CEOs to experiment with all types of BMI to operate more effectively in a VUCA world.
9. Taran et al. (2022).
10. Lego Ideas (2024).
11. Botoric (2015).
12. LEGO Serious Play® (2024).
13. McCusker and Swan (2018).
14. Pinault and Burleson (2007).
15. Warnerbros (2024).
16. Walt Disney (2024).
17. License Global (2024).
18. LEGO Newsroom (2019).
19. LEGO® DC Games (2024).
20. Prestige (2023).
21. LEGO-NASA (2024).
22. NASA (2024).
23. NASA-LEGO (2024).
24. LEGOLAND Parks (2024).
25. Merlin Entertainments (2024).
26. LEGO Ventures (2024).
27. Magretta (2002).
28. Amit and Zott (2001).
29. Chesbrough (2006), IBM (2006).
30. Taran et al. (2022).
31. The concept of zooming-in and zooming-out through various levels of operation (micro, meso, macro) has become a powerful metaphor in multiple fields, including BMI studies. It encapsulates the idea of shifting perspectives between detailed and broad holistic view analysis, helping understand the bigger picture and the detailed relation within and between components of a system. Abstracting offers a comprehensive understand-

ing of the complex interplay between various elements and their impact on overall performance, ways of organizing, and introducing new value-creation possibilities (Gordijn et al., 2005; Taran et al., 2022).
32. Taran et al. (2022).
33. Taran et al. (2022).
34. Skarzynski and Gibson (2008).
35. Osterwalder et al. (2005)); Lambert (2015)); Massa and Tucci (2013). For example, Osterwalder et al. (2005) differentiate between meta-models of BMs, taxonomies of BM types, modeled instances of BMs, and real-life firms. Massa and Tucci (2013) identify six levels of BM abstraction: activity systems, meta-models, specified graphical frameworks, ontologies, architypes, and narratives.
36. BM/BMI literature is still evolving to understand and conceptualize the levels and modes of abstracting. For examples of extant developments, see Massa and Tucci (2013); Osterwalder et al. (2005); Taran et al. (2022).
37. Gordijn et al. (2005), Taran et al. (2022).
38. According to Baden-Fuller and Morgan (2010), the process of configuration encompasses two models: *role models* and *scale models*. Role models offer brief depictions of actual BMs (e.g., "eBay" BM), while scale models present a general mode of operation. Given its wide adoption in the literature (Gassmann et al., 2014) and building on Taran et al. (2016), we categorize BM configurations using the terminology of scale models.
39. Fielt (2014), Taran et al. (2016, 2022).
40. Understanding how firms change and reconfigure their BM patterns or configurations is well established in the literature. For example, Gassmann et al. (2014) present a list of 55 BM configurations that were analyzed based on a four-dimensional framework encompassing value proposition, value chain, profit mechanism, and target customer. Building on Gassmann et al. (2014), Taran et al. (2016) designed a more comprehensive and structural framework for identifying up-to-date BM configurations, 71 in total, to aid practitioners in selecting suitable patterns for BMI.
41. Taran et al. (2016).
42. Chesbrough and Rosenbloom (2002), Osterwalder and Pigneur (2010).
43. Chesbrough and Rosenbloom (2002).
44. Chesbrough and Rosenbloom (2002), Stähler (2002).
45. Chesbrough and Rosenbloom (2002), Hamel (2000), Osterwalder and Pigneur (2010).
46. Baden-Fuller and Haefliger (2013), Baden-Fuller and Morgan (2010), Chesbrough and Rosenbloom (2002), Osterwalder and Pigneur (2010).
47. Spotify (2019).
48. Linder and Cantrell (2000).
49. Osterwalder and Pigneur (2010).

50. Johnson (2010).
51. Chesbrough (2006).
52. Osterwalder and Pigneur (2010).
53. Osterwalder and Pigneur (2010).
54. Amit and Zott (2001), Chesbrough (2010), IBM (2006), Magretta (2002), Taran et al. (2022), Teece (2010).

REFERENCES

Amit, R., & Zott, C. (2001). Value creation in e-business. *Strategic Management Journal, 22*(6-7), 493–520.

Baden-Fuller, C., & Haefliger, S. (2013). Business models and technological innovation. *Long Range Planning, 46*(6), 419–426.

Baden-Fuller, C., & Morgan, M. S. (2010). Business models as models. *Long Range Planning, 43*(2), 156–171.

Botoric, V. (2015). When ideas generate value: How LEGO profitably democratized its relationship with fans. In N. Zagalo & P. Branco (Eds.), *Creativity in the digital age*. Springer Series on Cultural Computing. Springer, London.

Casadesus-Masanell, R., & Ricart, J. E. (2010). From strategy to business models and onto tactics. *Long Range Planning, 43*(2), 195–215.

Chesbrough, H. (2006). *Open business models. How to thrive in the new innovation landscape*. Harvard Business School, Boston.

Chesbrough, H. (2010). Business model innovation: Opportunities and barriers. *Long Range Planning, 43*(2–3), 354–363.

Chesbrough, H., & Rosenbloom, R. S. (2002). The role of the business model in capturing value from innovation: Evidence from Xerox Corporation's technology spinoff companies. *Industrial and Corporate Change, 11*(3), 529–555.

Fielt, E. (2014). Conceptualising business models: Definitions, frameworks, and classifications. *Journal of Business Models, 1*(1), 85–105.

Gassmann, H., Frankenberger, K., & Csik, M. (2014). *The business model navigator*. Pearson Education Limited.

Gordijn, J., Osterwalder, A., & Pigneur, Y. (2005). Comparing two business model ontologies for designing e-business models and value constellations. Paper presented at the 18th conference *eIntegration in Action*, Bled, June 6–8.

Hamel, G. (2000). *Leading the revolution*. Harvard Business School Press.

IBM. (2006). Expanding the innovation horizon. Retrieved November 22, 2006, from https://t.ly/fkD4S

IBM. (2010). Capitalizing on complexity: Insights from the global chief executive officer study. Retrieved August 1, 2013, from https://t.ly/fSvWX

Johnson, M. W. (2010). *Seizing the white space: Business model innovation for growth and renewal*. Harvard Business Press.

Lambert, S. (2015). The importance of classification to business model research. *Journal of Business Models, 3*(1), 49–61.

Leifer, R. (2002). *Critical factors predicting radial innovation success.* Rensselaer Polytechnic Institute.

LEGO® DC Games. (2024). Take it to the next level with LEGO® DC Games. Retrieved April 30, 2024 from https://t.ly/wXHrH

Lego Ideas. (2024). *Lego ideas.* Retrieved April 30, 2024 from https://t.ly/QcHyI

LEGOLAND Parks. (2024). Legolandparks.com. Retrieved April 30, 2024 from https://t.ly/qg6xe

LEGO-NASA collaboration. (2021). NASA and the LEGO group: Building decades of collaboration. Retrieved April 30, 2024 from https://t.ly/cB2QK

LEGO Newsroom. (2019). LEGO group partners with Warner Bros. Consumer products to announce first-ever LEGO® building sets inspired by classic animated series Scooby-Doo™. Retrieved April 30, 2024 from https://t.ly/j5YDn

LEGO Ventures. (2024). LEGOVentures.com. Retrieved April 30, 2024 from https://t.ly/I3qAr

LEGO Serious Play®. (2024). LEGO® SERIOUS PLAY®. Retrieved April 30, 2024 from https://t.ly/KPIHn

License Global. (2018). LEGO and Warner Bros. *Build on Hobbit, Lord of the Rings.* Retrieved April 30, 2024 from https://t.ly/3pf-P

License Global. (2024). LEGO and Warner Bros. build Hobbit, Lord of the Rings. Retrieved April 30, 2024, from https://t.ly/3pf-P

Linder, J., & Cantrell, S. (2000). *Changing business models: Surveying the landscape.* Accenture Institute for Strategic Change.

Magretta, J. (2002). Why business models matter? *Harvard Business Review, 80*(5), 86–92.

Massa, L., & Tucci, C. L. (2013). Business model innovation. In M. Dodgson, D. M. Gann, & N. Phillips (Eds.), *The Oxford handbook of innovation management* (pp. 420–441). Oxford University Press.

McCusker, S., & Swan, J. C. (2018). The use of metaphors with LEGO® SERIOUS PLAY® for harmony and innovation. *International Journal of Management and Applied Research, 5*(4), 174–192.

Merlin Entertainmaint. (2024). Merlinentertainmaint.com. Retrieved April 30, 2024 from https://t.ly/IzC_M

NASA. (2024). Partnering with NASA STEM Engagement. Retrieved April 30, 2024 from https://t.ly/QWcnU

NASA-LEGO collaboration (2024). Build To Launch With LEGO Education and Artemis I. Retrieved April 30, 2024 from https://t.ly/ZQkm6

Osterwalder, A., & Pigneur, Y. (2010). *Business model generation: A handbook for visionaries, game changers, and challengers.* John Wiley and Sons.

Osterwalder, A., Pigneur, Y., & Tucci, L. C. (2005). Clarifying business models: Origins, present, and future of the concept. *Communications of AIS, 6*, 1–25.

Pinault, L., & Burleson, W. (2007). Collective innovation for Lunar exploration: Using LEGO® Robotics, 'Serious Games' and virtual reality to involve a massive number of players in direct, tele-operated surface activities. Retrieved April 30, 2024.

Prestige. (2023). LEGO X BTS and 7 other most iconic LEGO collaborations of all time. Retrieved April 30, 2024 from https://t.ly/qGBLs

Rosenstand, C. A. F., Brix, J., & Nielsen, C. (2023). Metaverse and Society 5.0: Pivotal for future business model innovation. *Journal of Business Models, 11*(3), 62–76.

Skarzynski, P., & Gibson, R. (2008). *Innovation to the core.* Harvard Business School Publishing.

Spotify. (2019). Spotify: Disrupting the global music industry. Retrieved May 10, 2024 from https://t.ly/OAttG

Stähler, P. (2002). Business models as a unit of analysis for strategizing. Paper presented at the 1st International Workshop on Business Models, Lausanne, Switzerland, October 4–5.

Taran, Y., Boer, H., & Nielsen, C. (2022). *The business model innovation process: Preparation, organization and management.* Routledge.

Taran, Y., Nielsen, C., Montemari, M., Thomsen, P., & Paolone, F. (2016). Business model configurations: A five-V framework to map out potential innovation routes. *European Journal of Innovation Management, 19*(4), 492–527.

Teece, D. J. (2010). Business models, business strategy and innovation. *Long Range Planning, 43*(2), 172–194.

Tidd, J., & Bessant, J. (2009). *Managing innovation: Integrating technological, market and organizational change.* John Wiley & Sons.

Warner Brothers. (2024). Warnerbrothers.com. Retrieved April 30, 2024 from https://t.ly/6HfWJ

Walt Disney. (2024). *The Walt Disney Company.* Retrieved April 30, 2024 from https://t.ly/qUwPR

CHAPTER 6

BMI and De-internationalization

The coast was a rugged one without a haven anywhere and there was nothing he feared quite so much in a storm as a lee shore.
—Seneca

6.1 Anchoring in Calm Waters

"As a rule, ... loss of ground and lack of fresh reserves are the two main reasons for retreat. There may, however, be others, which we do not wish to exclude or minimize, having to do with the interdependence of the parts or with the overall plan."[1] Although cross-border activities of firms are far from being about "mutual destruction,"[2] they are as much about competing parts of firms' cross-border gestalts (pattern, capacity, and logic) as about competing interdependencies of these parts. In the face of critical events, they are also about knowing "how" to reconfigure these interdependencies and equally important knowing not only "why" and "when" to reconfigure these interdependencies but also "when" to "retreat," partially or totally. During these critical events, the "blinds" can be and remain shut for various reasons, such as "an illusion of invulnerability that becomes shared by most members of the group" or "collective attempts to ignore or rationalize away items of information which might

© The Author(s), under exclusive license to Springer Nature Switzerland AG 2025
J. C. Sort et al., *De-internationalization and Re-internationalization of the Firm*,
https://doi.org/10.1007/978-3-031-81774-8_6

otherwise lead the group to reconsider shaky but cherished assumptions."[3] Indeed, "the difficulty of seeing things correctly ... makes things appear quite different from what was expected."[4]

When the "blinds *are* open," the firm may decide to "retreat" or de-internationalize due to changing market conditions, economic downturns, stringent regulatory environments, geopolitical instability, industrial competitive landscape, or internal pressures (see Chap. 3). Whether withdrawal is partial or total, it has a significant impact on the operating BMs of the firms. Withdrawal from international markets calls for BMI, reevaluation of interdependencies of its cross-border gestalt, operating BMs and value drivers, and, in some cases, even demand a complete transformation of existing BMs to ensure that firms remain competitive and have financial stability. BMI is a key to a successful de-internationalization to help firms, inter alia, reconfigure their supply chains, reallocate and/or revise the use of their resources. The 5-V framework (see Chap. 5) can be employed to support de-internationalization, for example:

- *Value Proposition*: The firm can streamline the withdrawing product/service line offerings with remaining customer needs for delivering unique value at home or abroad.
- *Value Segment*: The firm can rethink the segmentation of its international markets or regions and focus on targeting the most profitable ones to withstand de-internationalization. Despite its de-internationalization footprint, firms can maintain and even strengthen further their presence at home or in other international markets (re-internationalize).
- *Value Configuration*: This is probably the most affected value driver, which calls for functional and operational retrenchments, due to the downsizing of operations and reducing specific functions, including, for example, manufacturing, R&D, customer service, human capital, new distribution channels, and financial (which directly influences the firm's cost structure). De-internationalization can involve focusing on the core competencies of the firm and the simplification of its offering portfolio, by optimizing resource allocation and cutting non-essential activities, to ensure ongoing profitability efficiency and effectiveness.
- *Value Network*: The firm can re-evaluate current alliances, joint ventures, leasing, franchising, and other equity-mode and non-equity-

mode agreements. As part of a retrenchment partnership strategy, new possible network relations (or re-negotiated terms) could be forged in local markets, e.g., moving from a joint venture toward a license agreement.

- *Value Capture*: The firm can seek alternative revenue sources by adjusting, for example, its international price mix strategy (to compensate for lost revenue), enhance or revise its value capture capabilities.

Examining de-internationalization through the five value drivers will allow firms to strategically and systematically review and innovate their BMs, develop and adopt de-internationalization footprints (Fig. 1.2). For the purpose of this book, we focus on the link between the "hows" and "whys" of de-internationalization and the 5-V framework.

6.2 The "hows" of De-internationalization and BM Value Drivers

Understanding de-internationalization through BMI involves a comprehensive and systemic re-evaluation of value drivers individually and jointly with other drivers. Table 6.1 presents an example of a link between the types and "hows" of de-internationalization[5] (see Chap. 3) and BM value drivers[6] (see Chap. 5), highlighting various de-internationalization strategies and respective BM value drives that are directly affected by de-internationalization.

As we conjecture in Table 6.1, value configuration, value capture, and value segment drivers are mostly affected during de-internationalization, while value network drivers are affected to a lesser degree. In most instances of de-internationalization, the value proposition will not be affected, as the firm continues to operate in the home market, unless specialized offerings are still being offered in the de-internationalized markets. Partial withdrawal through a de-franchising strategy directly impacts the **value network, value configurations, and value capture**, necessitating innovations in how firms manage and leverage these relationships to maintain a market presence and strengthen operational efficiency and profitability. Partial withdrawal strategies that aim to combine domestic and international activities, such as offshoring, near-shoring, and decoupling highlight the need for flexibility and adaptability in firms' global

Table 6.1 De-internationalization "hows" and BM value drivers

De-internationalization types	The "hows" of de-internationalization	BM value drivers directly affected
Partial Withdrawal: *Optimizing Exit Modes*	*De-franchising*: reevaluating or terminating (contracting out) franchise agreements	**Value network** **Value configurations** **Value capture**
	De-licensing: ending/adjusting licensing agreements for enhancing control and profitability	**Value segment** **Value capture**
	De-exporting: reducing/ceasing exporting to shift focus toward either domestic/new (more profitable) markets	**Value segment** **Value configurations** **Value capture**
Partial Withdrawal: *Optimizing Foreign Markets*	*Offshoring*: moving to, e.g., low-cost countries/destinations for enhancing efficiency and cost competitiveness of global supply chain	**Value configurations** **Value segment** **Value capture**
	Near-shoring: moving to nearby countries to improve supply chain resilience, e.g, logistics and reduce transportation costs	**Value configurations** **Value capture**
	De-coupling: to increase flexibility, separating independent operational models for domestic and international operations for different markets, e.g., hybrid shoring strategic reorientation, combining offshoring, nearshoring, and backshoring	**Value configurations** **Value segment** **Value capture**

Partial Withdrawal: *Optimizing Operations*	*Downsizing*: operational retrenchment strategy and streamlining operations by cutting back on various operational activities to re-focus on core areas, e.g., staff, investment	Value configuration Value capture
	Product line rationalization: focus on offerings, streamlining, aimed for high margins and operational complexity reductions	Value proposition Value segment
	Functional retrenchment: maintain critical capabilities by reducing specific functions, e.g., R&D, customer service	Value configuration
	Renegotiation of terms: re-design flexible contract terms, allowing dynamic adjustments that would fit better for changing market conditions, e.g., strategic alliances dissolution to balance collaboration and independence	Value network Value configuration Value capture
	License back: license termination in one global location and return (back) to local licensing entity	Value network Value configuration Value capture
	Joint venture adjustment: adoption and modification of joint venture terms and global operational activities	Value network Value configuration Value capture
	Asset leasing: asset management through, e.g., leasing, rather than selling out (while de-internationalizing) owned property and equipment in foreign markets. Keeping the option to return-fast if and when the circumstances changes	Value configuration Value capture
	Financial restructuring and currency risk: de-internationalize to enhance financial stability by restructuring various financial aspects, e.g., currency (instability) risks, debt refinancing, investment strategies	Value capture
	Expatriate reduction and/or remote management: human resource strategies that focus on reducing the number of employees/management who were sent from the home country to work in foreign subsidiaries or operations	Value configuration Value capture
	Regulatory compliance reduction: de-internationalize from markets with strict and often comprehensive rules and laws regulations to increase operational flexibility	Value configuration Value capture
Total Withdrawal *Significant BM rethinking*	*Asset sale*: ceasing trading entirely in foreign markets (e.g., divesting (selling or closing) foreign subsidiaries or business units)	From few drivers (e.g., value network; value configuration; value capture) To all value drivers

supply chain, and underscore the importance of optimizing operations (e.g., value configuration) by balancing cost efficiency with logistical effectiveness. In this way, firms can enhance their supply chain resilience[7] and responsiveness to market changes.

6.3 The "Whys" of De-internationalization and BM Value Drivers

Understanding the link between the "whys" of de-internationalization (see Chap. 3) and BM value drivers[8] (see Chap. 5) is pivotal for successful BMI and adoption of de-internationalization exit modes (see Chap. 3 and Table 6.1). It can also assist decision-makers with re-internationalization decisions (see Chap. 7). In Table 6.2, we offer examples of possible links between the "whys" of de-internationalization and BM value drivers. These examples are to inspire the conceptualization of this relation and to identify respective interdisciplinary questions, rather than offer normative solutions.

Here is an example of a conceptualization of the "whys" of de-internationalization and BM value drivers. There could be an overlap between de-internationalization drivers and several BM value driver categories; these are highlighted in italics in the table. The "*decreased quality/profitability of the offer*" driver can be found in all BM value driver categories. It might be attributed to the value of the product/service itself, related to the value proposition. It may also be due to a shift in or misalignment with customers' preferences. If this is the case, then "*decreased quality/profitability of the offer*" could be attributed to a problem with the value segment. It could be that the product/service is simply not profitable, in this case, there might be an issue with the profit formula and value capture. Another reason could be an issue with a strategic shift in or conflict with a current partner (e.g., joint venture, strategic alliance, outsourced activity). This will direct the firm to look for a solution in its value network. If "*decreased quality/profitability of the offer*" were attributed to, for example, ordering or manufacturing processes, marketing and sales efforts, increasing costs, and/or loss of a core competency (e.g., IPR) in the market, then it would be attributed to value configuration. The sections below offer a more nuanced view of the intersection.

Table 6.2 The "whys" of de-internationalization and BM value drivers

Reasons to de-internationalize	BM value drivers
Decreased quality/profitability of the offer Increased attractiveness of the home market Maturity of the product in the target market Changes in national legal and normative environments (exchange rates, tariffs, inflation, and ownership structures)	Value proposition
Decreased quality/profitability of the offer Increased attractiveness of the home market Cultural difference/physical distance Changes in national legal and normative environments (exchange rates, tariffs, inflation, ownership structures)	Value segment
Intangible assets (both quality and quantity) *Change of ownership* *Decreased quality/profitability of the offer* *Lack of innovation* *Lack of international experience* *Lack of technological/technical capabilities* *New, more efficient production/technology* *Underperforming subsidiaries* Cultural difference/physical distance Increased production and transportation costs Lack in or poor performance of suppliers or distributors Quality and availability of labor Changes in national legal and normative environments (exchange rates, tariffs, inflation, and ownership structures)	Value configuration
New, more efficient production/technology *Decreased quality/profitability of the offer* Collaboration constraints (OEMs and VCs) Cultural difference/physical distance Lack in or poor performance of suppliers [other partners] or distributors Quality and availability of labor Changes in national legal and normative environments (exchange rates, tariffs, inflation, and ownership structures)	Value network
Decreased quality/profitability of the offer *Underperforming subsidiaries* Increased production and transportation costs Changes in national legal and normative environments (exchange rates, tariffs, inflation, and ownership structures)	Value capture

6.3.1 Linking the "whys" of De-internationalization to Value Proposition

The value proposition is a firm's offer of products and/or services that satisfy customer needs for which customers are willing to pay.[9] An example can be found in Rolls Royce engines, wherein Rolls Royce is selling the performance of the engines, rather than selling the engines directly, for example, to airlines. This means that airlines are "paying by the hour" only when the engines are working. In this way, Rolls Royce can keep track of engines and ensure quality and safety.[10] This can be viewed as changing the value proposition from product to service.[11] If "*decreased quality/profitability of the offer*" drives de-internationalization and the firm identifies slowing or decreasing demand for its offerings as one of the main issues, this could be linked to the value proposition driver. In this case, it is important for decision-makers to understand, inter alia, which features are misaligned with the expectations of the customers (Vignette 6.1). What is it that the customers are searching for that is currently not achieved? Is it about performance, reliability, durability, design, availability, and/or customization of the product/service? An important aspect of this link is to get a thorough understanding of the potential misalignment between the offerings of the firm and the expectations of the customers and a clear view of the reason(s) that led to de-internationalization. One way of re-aligning can be to sell the product performance instead of selling the product directly.

> **Vignette 6.1 International market exit—misaligned value perception**
> Firm A has encountered challenges in its international market, leading to the complete withdrawal of its wholly owned subsidiary from that market. It seeks to understand the underlying causes of this situation. The analysis of the situation indicates that its customers in that foreign market could not see "value-for-money" or correlation between the value of the firm offering and the associated costs. This led its customers to search for alternative options. This outcome was unexpected for the firm, as, in the view of the firm, the pricing of its offering was consistent with the price range in its foreign and local market. The firm came to realize that price and perceived value can vary significantly across different markets.
>
> (*continued*)

> **Vignette 6.1 (continued)**
>
> In this case, one of the main concerns can be defined as a "*decreased profitability of the offer*," which relates to the "*value proposition*" value driver. In other words, should the firm choose to enter this foreign market again, at a later stage, it should further examine its value proposition and how customers perceive the value of its offering to better understand the price-value match. Further investigation into the reasons behind this de-internationalization is, thus, necessary and may generate new possible solutions in a later phase. For instance, a deeper analysis of the firm's value configuration could explore where operating costs could be reduced, or whether outsourcing production activities to low-cost countries might be considered. Each of these options would have BMI implications.

6.3.2 Linking the "whys" of De-internationalization to Value Segment

The value segment is a customer segment (or segments) a firm aims to serve and how the firm intends to establish relationships with customers.[12] For example, McDonald's needed to change their product when entering the Indian market, as its best-selling menu item, the "Big Mac," consists of a burger with beef patties. The cow being a spiritual animal in India, the firm needed to change its products and menu to focus on chicken instead.[13] If "*cultural difference/physical distance*" drives de-internationalization and assuming the firm at the time of de-internationalization has profitable sales in its home market, it might want to investigate why international customers are not reacting in the same way. Is it due to different cultural values in the foreign market and the domestic market? A value offering satisfying one demographic customer segment will not necessarily satisfy another demographic segment in a different country/region. Is it because of different expectations toward customer-firm relationships? It might be that the customers in the foreign market expect different interactions or relationships with the firm in the process of building loyalty and/or trust (e.g., in-person vs. digital relations, assistance and support rather than DIY and self-service).

6.3.3 Linking the "whys" of De-internationalization to Value Configuration

The value configuration is a mix of key resources that enable a firm's key activities that create, produce, and deliver the value proposition effectively to the target value segments.[14] An example of this can be Tupperware that adopted a direct selling model, relying on a network of independent sales consultants rather than big retailers.[15] If *"increased production and/or transportation costs"* drives de-internationalization, the firm needs to investigate how and in what way this reason affected its choice to de-internationalize. Assuming that the increased costs could not be transferred to the customers (e.g., due to a price increase), is the problem then mainly attributed to higher costs when serving this specific foreign market, or is it a general problem in all operating markets—global and domestic? Are the costs related to any capacity constraint (e.g., equipment, poor reliability, utilities, planning, space, HR, materials shortages)? Is the increase in costs leading to a lesser offering attractiveness or competitiveness? Should the firm launch an audit of its resources, activities, and distribution channels to make sure the value offering is cost-effectively served to the customers and the cost structure is streamlined when developing a revised re-internationalization strategy?

> **Vignette 6.2 International market exit—challenges in achieving economies of scale**
>
> Firm B has encountered difficulties in its international market and withdrew from that market via a "functional retrenchment" strategy that allowed the firm to maintain its critical capabilities in this market, such as R&D and customer service, but led to the closure of its production facilities there. Although initial entry was successful, the firm failed to turn a profit due to an expected and sudden increase in operating costs. The increased costs stemmed from the need to purchase additional parts to repair their production equipment and machines, along with higher costs for delivering local supplier parts to this foreign market. These increased costs cannot always be transferred to customers, so the firm had to explore alternative strategies to remain profitable.

(continued)

Vignette 6.2 (continued)
It could be argued that the "why" behind this withdrawal is related to the "increased production and/or transportation costs." This might require an investigation into the firm's internal structure (or other components of its "capacity") and the development of a revised operating BM to enhance the efficiency and effectiveness of utilized activities and resources (its capacity). While many firms expect to achieve economies of scale or scope relatively easily when expanding into new foreign markets, realizing this can be challenging due to unexpected challenges or shocks that may arise.

6.3.4 Linking the "whys" of De-internationalization to Value Network

The value network is a network of partners who engage in different types of cooperation with the firm to achieve economies of scale or scope, risk reduction, or tap into new knowledge or resources.[16] An example can be found in Procter & Gamble, which opened up its business model to more partnerships to boost its innovation and growth performance.[17] If "*lack in or poor performance of suppliers [re-sellers, other partners] or distributors*" drives de-internationalization, the firm needs to revisit its entire network, especially the "problematic" partners. To what extent does poor network performance or weak relationships or partnerships contribute to the de-internationalization choice? It could be an easy way out to "just find a new and better supplier/re-seller/partner," but there could be more fundamental internal or external reasons why the firm is locked-in and inflexible with its de-internationalization choices, e.g., in the context of relations that involve tight contractual agreements of supplier/distribution/re-seller exclusivity, a joint venture, outsourcing, or licensing agreements. The firm must audit its partner selection criteria, such as economies of scale, optimization, knowledge, acquisition of particular resources and activities, resources, and/or risk and/or uncertainty reduction.[18]

6.3.5 Linking the "whys" of De-internationalization to Value Capture

The value capture is about how and how much the customers pay for the delivered products or services.[19] Examples are Gillette or Nespresso that chose to rely on selling the primary product cheaper (razors/coffee machines) but continued to generate more revenues from the accessories (e.g., blades/coffee capsules refill), known as the "bait and hook" value capture.[20] If "*changes in national legal and normative environments*" drive de-internationalization, the firm needs to understand the context and nature of these changes, which could be related to exchange rates, tariffs, inflation, and/or ownership structures. In this instance, the firm should revisit how it captures the value of selling the product/service to the customer. Could it be possible for the firm to change some parts of its BM to accommodate these changes in the foreign market? Would it be possible to sell the product/service differently to accommodate the exchange rates or tariffs? Could the value be captured using a different revenue model? Or could a change in the ownership structure be a possible solution to accommodate the market's legal environment?

> **Vignette 6.3 Navigating market exit: pricing challenges in international markets**
>
> Firm C has faced difficulties in its international market due to new legislation or "changes in national legal and normative environments," which imposed an extra tax on its product, making it more expensive. Since its product is already positioned at the higher end of the industry price range, the increased costs led customers to question its "value-for-money" and uniqueness compared to alternative offerings, resulting in decreased demand. By zooming-in on its operating BM, the firm tries to find ways to stay in the market by absorbing the additional costs in house and looking for additional ways to optimize further production processes; renegotiating suppliers' contracts; reevaluating the product design and features; offering additional complementary services to the core product (e.g., bait and hook strategy); and/or developing a new value capture model (e.g., price tiering or subscription-based options). At the same, by zooming-in, the firm discovered that the new tax substantially disrupted the balance of having customers willing to pay higher price based on perceived quality and uniqueness and it is going to persist. This assessment led the firm to fully de-internationalize.

6.4 Concluding Remarks

In this chapter, we made the first attempt to explore de-internationalization through the five value drivers. Specifically, we took a "slice" of the de-internationalization "pie" or pattern, namely, the "hows" and the "whys," to examine a firm's withdrawal through the lenses of the five value drivers. This allowed us to achieve at least two goals. On the one hand, within the scope of the chosen patterns of de-internationalization, "why" and "how," we identified various de-internationalization strategies and respective BM value drivers that were affected by intended de-internationalization, e.g., to optimize exit modes, foreign markets, operations or fundamentally redesign a firm's BM. On the other hand, we developed an approach about how BMI can be employed to help academics and non-academic research, make sense of de-internationalization through BMI lenses, including the five value drivers. This approach needs further refinement and development to account not only for the full pattern of de-internationalization gestalt but also its capacity and logic. It must also be able to account for partial and total withdrawal of the firm and de-internationalization errors, the error of commission (De-e1) and the error of omission (De-e2). It has to be able to explain how BMI strategies, abstracting, zooming-in, zooming-out, and iterating, can be employed to better understand and effect de-internationalization—"open the blinds and pull the plug"—to avoid failure, recover and even re-internationalize.

Notes

1. von Clausewitz (1989, p. 231).
2. von Clausewitz (1989, p. 236).
3. Dixon (1976, p. 399).
4. von Clausewitz (1997, p. 65).
5. Turcan (2006).
6. Taran et al. (2016, 2022).
7. Tukamuhabwa et al. (2015).
8. Taran et al. (2016, 2022).
9. Taran et al. (2016).
10. Smith (2013).
11. Johnson (2010).
12. Taran et al. (2016).
13. Nandini (2014).
14. Taran et al. (2016).

15. Tupperware (2024); Tupperware was one of the first to adopt this way of externalizing its sales force which led to having a salesforce of 2.3 million, where most were part-time involved. This was a strong configuration for Tupperware for many years. Recently, the company began to sell a selection of its products through Target (Pangarkar, 2015; Target, 2024).
16. Taran et al. (2016).
17. Chesbrough (2006), Osterwalder and Pigneur (2010). To achieve that, P&G developed the Connect and Develop (C&D) model, moving beyond pure R&D. In this way, they followed an open innovation strategy where they could leverage and couple their own R&D, manufacturing, marketing, and purchasing capabilities with their new partners, and introduce new lines of business brands (Huston & Sakkab, 2006; Taran et al., 2022).
18. Osterwalder and Pigneur (2010).
19. Taran et al. (2016).
20. Gassmann et al. (2014), Osterwalder and Pigneur (2010).

References

Dixon, N. (1976). *On the psychology of military incompetence*.
Gassmann, H., Frankenberger, K., & Csik, M. (2014). *The business model navigator*. Pearson Education Limited.
Huston, L., & Sakkab, N. (2006). Connect and develop: Inside Procter & Gamble's new model for innovation. *Harvard Business Review, 84*(3), 58–67.
Johnson, M. W. (2010). *Seizing the white space: Business model innovation for growth and renewal*. Harvard Business Press.
Nandini, A. S. (2014). McDonald's success story in India. *Journal of Contemporary Research in Management, 9*(3), 21.
Osterwalder, A., & Pigneur, Y. (2010). *Business model generation: A handbook for visionaries, game changers, and challengers*. John Wiley and Sons.
Pangarkar, N. (2015). Performance implications of strategic changes: An integrative framework. *Business Horizons, 58*(3), 295–304.
Smith, D. J. (2013). Power-by-the-hour: The role of technology in reshaping business strategy at Rolls-Royce. *Technology Analysis & Strategic Management, 25*(8), 987–1007.
Taran, Y., Boer, H., & Nielsen, C. (2022). *The business model innovation process: Preparation, organization and management*. Routledge.
Taran, Y., Nielsen, C., Montemari, M., Thomsen, P., & Paolone, F. (2016). Business model configurations: A five-V framework to map out potential innovation routes. *European Journal of Innovation Management, 19*(4), 492–527.

Target Brands. (2024). Tupperware. Retrieved March 5, 2024, from https://t.ly/LdJVo

Tukamuhabwa, B. R., Stevenson, M., Busby, J., & Zorzini, M. (2015). Supply chain resilience: Definition, review and theoretical foundations for further study. *International Journal of Production Research*, 53(18), 5592–5623.

Tupperware. (2024). Retrieved April 15, 2024, from https://t.ly/-I4kV

Turcan, R. V. (2006). De-internationalization of small high-technology firms: An international entrepreneurship perspective. Doctoral dissertation, University of Strathclyde, Glasgow, UK.

Von Clausewitz, C. (1989). *On victory and defeat: From on war*. Princeton University Press.

Von Clausewitz, C. (1997). *On war*. Wordsworth Editions Ltd.

CHAPTER 7

BMI and Re-internationalization

Miracles are explainable; it is the explanations that are miraculous.
—Tim Robinson

7.1 Setting a New Voyage

"You can't step twice in the same river" warned Heraclitus. But firms do "step in" and return to internationalization. A key question is whether it is the "same river." Series of concerns are to be addressed for re-internationalization to happen and be successful. Why, and equally important how, to "step in" again, revive outward cross-border activities after de-internationalization. What was learned, what was unlearned in the process? What is the new dominant BM logic that must be adopted to re-internationalize? What BMI opportunities exist to innovate the firm re-internationalization pattern (e.g., how, why, when, what, where, who), capacity (e.g., resources, capabilities, processes, structures, strategies, motivation), and logic? What is the most optimal value driver and BM configuration to achieve target re-internationalization effects? From this myriad of questions, we will address the following questions in this chapter. What are the "hows" of re-internationalization? How the "whys" of de-internationalization, moderated by BMI, can inform the modes, or

© The Author(s), under exclusive license to Springer Nature Switzerland AG 2025
J. C. Sort et al., *De-internationalization and Re-internationalization of the Firm*,
https://doi.org/10.1007/978-3-031-81774-8_7

"hows," of re-internationalization? And, how five value drivers and BM configurations can moderate de-internationalization and re-internationalization (Fig. 1.2)?

7.2 The "Hows" of Re-internationalization and BMI Types

When re-internationalizing, firms do have at their disposal the same set of foreign market entry modes as when internationalizing. We conjecture that a key difference between the two approaches to the foreign market entry modes is the way BMI types (see Chap. 5) are employed to better understand, conceptualize, and innovate a foreign market *re-entry* mode (Table 7.1). There could be many (re-)*internationalization pattern* routes, each of which calls for different (re-)*internationalization capacity*[1] and *logic*, where the organizational processes, resource, and capability base (e.g., technological, human, and financial) will need to be amended to fit each internationalization pattern selected.

Table 7.1 Foreign market (re-)entry modes and BMI

Foreign market entry modes[a]	Description	BMI types
Exporting	Direct exporting "…a company final or intermediate product is manufactured outside the target country and subsequently transferred to it" Indirect exporting "uses middlemen who are located in the company's own country and who actually do the exporting"[b]	Closed: Inside-in BMI
Greenfield investments	Describes "a company or an area of business that is completely new"[c]	Closed: Inside-in BMI
Brownfield investments	"An area in a town or city that has been used in the past for factories or offices, and that could now be used for new building development"[d]	Closed: Inside-in BMI
Acquisition	"The act of buying something such as a company, a building, or a piece of land"[e]	(Semi) closed: Open, outside-in BMI
Merger	"An occasion when two or more companies or organizations join together to make one larger company"[f]	(Semi) closed: Open, outside-in BMI

(*continued*)

Table 7.1 (continued)

Foreign market entry modes[a]	Description	BMI types
Licensing	"A company transfers to a foreign entity (usually smother company) for a defined period of time the right to use its individual property (patents, know how, or trademarks) in return for a royalty or other compensation"[g]	(Semi) closed, Open, outside-in BMI (licensing-in another firm's IP) Open inside-out BMI (licensing-out the firm's IP to a third party) Open: Inside-out/ outside-in BMI (the above examples take place simultaneously)
Franchising	"Differs from licensing in motivation, services, and duration. In addition to granting the right to use the company name, trademarks, and technology, the franchisor also assists the franchisee in organization, marketing, and general management under an arrangement intended to be permanent"[h]	(Semi) closed, open outside-In, BMI (as franchisee) Open: Inside-out BMI (as franchisor)
Strategic alliances	"A collaborative agreement is any inter-organizational agreement, with or without equity, that involves the bilateral or multiparty contribution or exchange of assets or their services"[i]	Open: Inside-out/ outside-in BMI (contract manufacturing, piggybacking) Network level BMI
Joint Ventures	"Ownership and control shared between the parent company and one or more local partners, who usually represent a local company"[j]	Open: Inside-out BMI Open: Outside-in BMI
Born-global[k]	"Business organizations that, from inception, seek to derive significant competitive advantage from the use of resources and the sale of outputs in multiple countries"[l]	From scratch BMI

[a]Inspired by Root (1994)
[b]Root (1998, p. 7)
[c]Cambridge Dictionary
[d]Cambridge Dictionary
[e]Cambridge Dictionary
[f]Cambridge Dictionary
[g]Root (1998, p. 7)
[h]Root (1998, p. 7)
[i]Teece and Pisano (1987)
[j]Root (1998, p. 8)
[k]Although born global is not considered a market entry mode, we chose to include it in the list, since it represents a firm type that from its inception (i.e., from scratch) has a global market reach orientation
[l]Kudina et al. (2008)

7.3 THE "WHYS" OF RE-INTERNATIONALIZATION AND BM VALUE DRIVERS

7.3.1 Linking the "whys" of Re-internationalization to Value Proposition

If "d*ecreased quality/profitability of the offer*" drives de-internationalization of the firm due to a steady decrease in its offerings' demand, cheaper and lower quality competitive products, then the firm can adopt a "*no-frills*" BM configuration[2] to re-internationalize. By adopting a "*no frills*" BM configuration the firm would deliver a low(er)-cost version of its product/service, while maintaining the relevancy of the offerings. In the process, it might be beneficial to streamline the product/service down to its main core value. Cutting the cost of the product/service and introducing revised competitive pricing, while (hopefully) still maintaining the uniqueness and differentiation of the offer, may raise customers' demand and returns. An example of a "*no frills*" BM configuration is Ryanair, a budget airline with no extra add-ons, unless the customer is willing to pay more for additional services.[3]

7.3.2 Linking the "whys" of Re-internationalization to Value Segment

If "*cultural difference/physical distance*" drives de-internationalization, then the firm might want to explore how and why customers' perceptions, attitudes, and demands differ in its international markets and in the home market (Vignette 7.1). If this is due to "representativeness cognitive bias,"[4] where the firm incorrectly generalizes a decision from a small sample or one incident, then the firm might want to explore a "*customer-focused*" BM configuration to gain greater insights into its international customers and revise its re-internationalization strategy accordingly. This might result in opening a sales office in a foreign target market. A relevant, re-internationalization example is needed. If de-internationalization in this instance is due to a misfit between the foreign target market and the design of the offering in that market (e.g., the offer is overpriced, the target market has low purchasing power), then the firm may adopt a "*target the poor*" BM configuration as part of its re-internationalization strategy. Walmart adopted a "target the poor" BM configuration from its inception to offer low-priced products for the masses. The economy of scale is the basis of its profitability: it buys in bulk and receives discounts from its suppliers. Maintaining an efficient supply chain also enables Walmart to sell its offerings cheaply.[5]

Vignette 7.1 From failure to success: Effecting re-internationalization
Firm D is successful in its domestic market, branded as innovative, offering high-quality, low-cost, reliable products. A few years back, it launched its first internationalization strategy through direct exporting (Table 7.1), mirroring its successful domestic offerings portfolio. In several months since its international foreign market entry, the anticipated financial results did not materialize. The firm realized that it "fell into a trap" that many firms do, namely, "cultural difference/physical distance" (Table 6.2). It didn't sufficiently analyze the nuances of its selected foreign market, failing to understand customer behavior (e.g., values, lifestyle, purchasing patterns, and powers). The firm also realized that, although there might be a good alignment between its low-priced products and market demand, it failed short on its own to generate a profit margin to sustain its international growth strategy.

Following this unsuccessful attempt to internationalize, the firm decided to withdraw, de-export, from that market. It didn't give up. It tried to regroup, build on "learning from its mistakes," and develop a re-internationalization strategy. Series of lessons were identified. The firm realized that international expansion is not necessarily about replicating, "as-is," its domestic strategies. Instead, it is about aligning its offerings with the values and expectations of selected target markets. Finding a local partner to guide its market entry is critical for that target market rather than rely on direct exporting. Eventually, the firm designed a dual re-internationalization strategy to (1) "Target the poor," offering its products to the customers positioned at the base of the pyramid, and/or with low buying power; and (2) pursue a "Joint Venture," Open: Inside-out BMI, approach (Table 7.1).

The firm's decision to form a joint venture with a local partner allowed it to gain deeper insights into consumer behavior, cultural values, and the overall economic conditions of the foreign market. This approach enabled the firm to develop a new line of products that were better suited for meeting consumer expectations, ensuring a stronger product-market fit. Gradually, the results from re-entering the market allowed the firm to even expand further its international growth strategy to other markets with similar consumer behaviors.

(*continued*)

> **Vignette 7.1 (continued)**
> To achieve that, it used a flexible hybrid re-entry strategy to adapt to these diverse market's conditions effectively (Table 7.1), through:
>
> - *Direct exporting: Closed: Inside-in BMI*, this time, with a successful alignment between the new line of offerings and markets expectations. This approach was applied to markets with close resemblance and required minimal to no offering's adaptation.
> - *Licensing: Open: Inside-out BMI*, as the demand for its new line of product rose significantly, the firm chose to grant licensing rights for local firms to manufacture, market and sale their offerings under the firm's brand.
> - *Franchising: Open: Inside-out BMI*, by capitalizing on local retail expansion and local successful entrepreneurs, the firm established quickly a wide audience presence through its network and stores.
>
> This approach allowed the firm to employ various BMI types to tailor its entry modes to effectively match the unique characteristics of each (value segment) selected market.

7.3.3 Linking the "whys" of Re-internationalization to Value Configuration

If *"increased production and/or transportation costs"* drive de-internationalization, the firm could gain inspiration from a *"self-service"* BM configuration to re-internationalize. In this configuration, customers pay lower prices for the offer by performing several offer-related tasks themselves, contributing eventually to the firm's profitability. Some customers are willing to do a part themselves and still pay the same price or potentially a slightly smaller price, but the cost savings could be significant. Before adopting this configuration, the firm must, of course, investigate if customers are willing or happy to do *"self-service"* themselves. An example of successfully applying such a "self-service" BM configuration is IKEA. Its customers are expected to get the products themselves from the warehouses, they can check themselves out through self-service counters, and they have to assemble the furniture themselves at home.[6]

7.3.4 Linking the "whys" of Re-internationalization to Value Network

If "*lack in or poor performance of suppliers [re-sellers, other partners] or distributors*" drives de-internationalization, then the firm may revise its network, including the "problematic" partners. If the main problem is a lack of competent distributors or re-sellers, the firm may adopt and pursue as part of its re-internationalization strategy "*franchising*" BM configuration, where the seller has higher stakes and potentially a higher incentive to perform better (Vignette 7.2). An example of the application of such a configuration to strengthen its value network is Starbucks. Having firms buying into becoming a franchisee with a permit to use the brand and economy of scale but having to pay a percentage or fee to the franchise owner has proven successful in making Starbucks scale up rather fast and become one of the world's leading coffee shops.[7]

Vignette 7.2 There is always a way to re-internationalize
Firm E, a leader in its home market, decided to replicate its success internationally. Initially, it adopted a "Closed: Inside-in BMI" export entry mode (Table 7.1). In this process, it relied on local distributors and resellers in the foreign market to sell its products and offer its services. However, it quickly realized that something was not working as it should, as the sales volume was constantly lower than projected. To remedy the situation, the firm doubled the number of local distributors and resellers. Unfortunately, sales volume continued to decline. Eventually, the firm decided to de-internationalize.

The analysis of the situation revealed that the problem was not with its products and services as customers were satisfied with the firm products and services they purchased. Instead, the problem was a "lack in or poor performance of suppliers [re-sellers, other partners] or distributors" (linking this to the "value network"). Local distributors and sellers simply failed to meet the firm's expectations. Diving into the "kernel" of the problem, it emerged that distributors lacked the commitment and motivation to promote the firm's products, often prioritizing competing brands that offered them better incentives. Following up on these findings and being

(*continued*)

Vignette 7.2 (continued)

committed to re-internationalize, the firm compared and contrasted several re-internationalization postures to make a better-informed, re-internationalization decision (Table 7.2).

Following this evaluation, Firm E identified *Franchising* as the most suitable re-internationalization strategy that offered a strong balance between maintaining control and motivating partners, while generating revenue through royalties. This time, the firm proceeded cautiously by piloting its new franchise model. It carefully selected a few franchisees and provide them with an extensive training program, ensuring they were knowledgeable not only on the product features but also about the firm's service and brand values. Eventually, the results of the pilot efforts were successful, and the firm decided to scale this growth model slowly and steadily in the target foreign market, as product visibility and sales continue to climb.

Table 7.2 Evaluating re-internationalization postures

Entry mode	Pros	Cons	Fit for firm E
Exporting	Easy market entry, accompanied by low investment risk	Over dependent, and partial (to no) control, over local distributors	Closed: Inside-in BMI. Initially used by Firm E, but failed, due to distributors poor performance and lack of market control.—*No fit*
Licensing	Easy market entry with minimal investment	Lower profit margins that involve partial control over offerings quality	Open: Inside-out BMI. Provides fast market entry but risk the firm offerings quality and overall brand.—*Marginal fit*
Greenfield Investments (Offshoring)	Keeping the strong brand by sustaining full control over operations, offerings quality, delivery, and sales	High risk, as it demands high capital investment, and a longer timeline for realizing return on investment, let alone a sustained profit margin	Closed: Inside-in BMI. Although appealing, this approach requires significant financial resources that Firm E does not have.—*No fit*

(*continued*)

Table 7.2 (continued)

Entry mode	Pros	Cons	Fit for firm E
Joint Venture	Gain access to local market knowledge and share investment risks	Requires significant resources investment, which the firm currently does not have. Additionally, given previous experience in that market, the firm is not interested in overcommitting and risking potential conflicts with a local partner	Open: Inside-out BMI. Although it offers local expertise and shared risk, it is currently considered over-complex option for Firm E.—Marginal fit
Franchising	Maintaining strong control over the brand and product, partners are better motivated, and their success generates revenue through royalties paid to Firm E	A slow process (for Firm E profile), which requires careful selection and training of selected franchisees. It will also involve signing various legal and contractual agreements with the new partners, but with less binding complexities than in the joint-venture option	Open: Inside-out BMI (as franchisor). This option is the preferred approach by the firm, as it ensures highly motivated partners that are committed and show common interest in the success of the brand.—*Best fit for Firm E*

7.3.5 Linking the "whys" of Re-internationalization to Value Capture

If "*changes in national legal and normative environments*" drive de-internationalization, affecting the ownership of the product or service held by the firm, decision-makers could adopt and pursue a "*fractionalization*" BM configuration as part of its re-internationalization strategy. This configuration allows customers (or potential partners) to own part of the product/service or shares of the firm, enjoying co-ownership cost and benefits, risks and responsibilities. This might circumvent some of the legal issues faced in the foreign market and enable the firm to continue and sell its offerings. A "*fractionalization*" BM configuration example is Mobility Carsharing targeting customers who are unhappy paying for a car they rarely used, but still would like the convenience of having the car available when the situational need occurs. Mobility Carsharing designed a business model scheme where people can either buy a car together if they live near each other, or they can have a subscription that enables them to lend a car when needed without having the running costs of owning the car themselves.[8]

7.4 A First Step Toward an IB-BM Framework

Building on the above discussion, we take the first step to link de-internationalization and re-internationalization via BMI. Specifically, to link the "whys" of de-internationalization with the "hows" of re-internationalization via BM value drivers and configurations. This allows us to start shaping—planting the seeds for—the initial IB-BMI framework (Table 7.3) that we will refine in the next chapter. This, middle-range, framework (Table 7.3) explores how de-internationalization (e.g., its "whys") can inform re-internationalization (e.g., its "hows") moderated

Table 7.3 A first step toward an IB-BM framework

The "whys" of de-internationalization	Value drivers	The "hows" of re-internationalization (informed by BM configurations)
Decreased quality/ profitability of the offer Increased attractiveness of the home market Maturity of the product in the target market Changes in national legal and normative environments (exchange rates, tariffs, inflation, and ownership structures)	Value proposition	Cool brands: Use high-end brand marketing for offerings, either singly or with expert partners Crowdsourcing: Attain services/ideas from external actors (e.g., online communities) who add information and create value for one another Full-service provider: Offer complete coverage of services in one area No frills: Offer low-cost, low-price services or products in a traditionally high-end offering industry Price reduction bundling: Package deal lowers the price sum of the single products/services Quality selling: High-quality products sold for premium prices (mostly R&D based) Trusted product/service leadership: Secure sustainable customer relationships through a continuous upgrade platform path User design: Customers design their creative products Value-added reseller: Offering a complete selection in a focus product category for attractive prices Value bundling: Offer a package of goods or services to form a single unique offering

(continued)

Table 7.3 (continued)

The "whys" of de-internationalization	Value drivers	The "hows" of re-internationalization (informed by BM configurations)
Decreased quality/profitability of the offer Increased attractiveness of the home market Cultural difference/physical distance Changes in national legal and normative environments (exchange rates, tariffs, inflation, ownership structures)	Value segment	Customer-focused: Pull from demand: focus on customer needs Multisided platforms: Facilitating interactions between two or more distinct but interdependent groups of customers Robinhood: Similar offerings are being sold at high prices to high-income customers but at lower prices to low-income customers Round up buyers: Purchase discounts and attractive prices are gained by rounding up buyers together Target the poor: The offering targets the customer positioned at the base of the pyramid
Intangible assets (both quality and quantity) Change of ownership Decreased quality/profitability of the offer Lack of innovation Lack of international experience Lack of technological/technical capabilities New, more efficient production/technology Underperforming subsidiaries Cultural difference/physical distance Increased production and transportation costs Lack in or poor performance of suppliers or distributors Quality and availability of labor Changes in national legal and normative environments (exchange rates, tariffs, inflation, and ownership structures)	Value configuration	(e)Procurement: Tendering procurement of goods or services Channel maximization: Multiple channels are used for product distribution to maximize the broadest reach possible Core focused: Focus on very core competencies of the firm and outsource all other activities Disintermediation: Deliver a product or service directly to the end customer External sales force: Aggressive external sales force motivated by pyramid commission structures, for example Integrator: Controlling all resources and capabilities needed to create value within a given value chain Reverse innovation: Cheap products created within and for emerging markets that are also repackaged and resold in developed nations Self-service: Customers gain lower prices by performing some value creation process tasks on their own Trade show: Outsource some value chain functions to a third party with a well-known brand name Trash to cash: Used products or materials are reused or recycled and sold as a new offering (sustainability-related) Branded reliable commodity: Well-designed brand marketing White label: An offering created by one firm is (re)packaged and sold by multiple marketers under varying brands

(continued)

Table 7.3 (continued)

The "whys" of de-internationalization	Value drivers	The "hows" of re-internationalization (informed by BM configurations)
New, more efficient production/technology *Decreased quality/ profitability of the offer* Collaboration constraints (OEMs and VCs) Cultural difference/ physical distance Lack in or poor performance of suppliers or distributors Quality and availability of labor Changes in national legal and normative environments (exchange rates, tariffs, inflation, and ownership structures)	Value network	Adaptive: Create a technology-based "ecosystem" platform for innovations and benefit from the investments of others on that platform Barter: Exchange of offerings are with no money transfer among partners due to a mutual benefit from bartering Crowdfunding: Financing of ideas is generated from the public Franchising: Being part of a big chain or brand Inside-out: Sell or license unused homegrown IPs Integrated: The firm operates as a system integrator by using external sources to fuel the business and allowing unused ideas and technologies to flow to the outside Outside-in: Gather value (e.g., IPs and information) from external innovation partners or other communities
Decreased quality/ profitability of the offer *Underperforming subsidiaries* Increased production and transportation costs Changes in national legal and normative environments (exchange rates, tariffs, inflation, and ownership structures)	Value capture	Bait and hook: Offering customers an inexpensive or free initial product and charging more for additional related products Fractionalization: Customers own part of a product and enjoy the benefit of ownership Freemium: Basic offerings are granted for free, and additional offerings require payment Leasing: Renting products rather than outright selling them Pay what you want: Pricing a given product or service is set by the customer Pay as you go: Customers are charged based on actual usage (metered services) Subscription club: Customers are charged based on a fixed subscription fee The long tail: Wide range of products are sold in low quantities Upfront payment: Customers pay upfront for their goods

Note: The list of BM configurations presented herein is not exhaustive (For a comprehensive list of BM configurations, see Chesbrough (2006), Gassmann et al. (2014), Johnson (2010), Linder and Cantrell (2000), Osterwalder and Pigneur (2010), Taran et al. (2016; 2021), Timmers (1998)). It serves as an inspiration regarding how BM value drivers and BM configurations can be interpreted to moderate de-internationalization and re-internationalization relationship. The internal drivers of de-internationalization are in italic. From left to right: reasons of de-internationalization are identified and assessed first. One or several de-internationalization reasons could be examined through several value drivers that offer decision-makers several BM configurations opportunities to consider how to re-internationalize through the lenses of BM value drivers and configurations as we conceptualized the relationship in Fig. 1.2. It is based on a conjecture that understanding the "whys" of de-internationalization through BM value drivers can inform BM configurations of re-internationalization ('hows" of re-internationalization), shaping its patterns and capacities. This emerging framework is designed as a practical, strategic learning toolkit available for firms to better understand, make sense of, their de-internationalization experience and get an inspiration of different avenues available for them to re-internationalize.

7.5 Concluding Remarks

In this chapter, we have offered an initial conceptual understanding of the relationship between re-internationalization and BMI and between re-internationalization and de-internationalization moderated through the lenses of BM value drivers and configurations. Specifically, we build on the two dimensions of the re-internationalization pattern, namely, its "whys" and "hows," to explore this relationship. Within the scope of this chapter, we also laid a foundation of how re-internationalization gestalt—pattern, capacity, and logic—can be assessed through the BMI lenses. Temporal and process dimensions of re-internationalization are equally important to understand their relationship with de-internationalization and internationalization: for example, how BMI can correct the two errors of re-internationalization, error of commission (Re-e1) and error of omission (Re-e2); or how BMI can inform re-internationalization strategies, imitating, balancing, rejuvenating, and taking time-off. At the same time, we have planted "seeds" for a future IB-BMI framework that we fully develop and discuss in the next chapter.

Notes

1. Petersen and Welch (2003), Welch and Luostarinen (1988).
2. Taran et al. (2016).
3. Casadesus and Ricart (2011).
4. Dane and Pratt (2007), Hill et al. (2016).
5. Brea-Solís et al. (2015).
6. IKEA (2024).
7. Gassmann et al. (2014).
8. Gassmann et al. (2014).

References

Brea-Solís, H., Casadesus-Masanell, R., & Grifell-Tatjé, E. (2015). Business model evaluation: Quantifying Walmart's sources of advantage. *Strategic Entrepreneurship Journal, 9*(1), 12–33.

Casadesus, R., & Ricart, J. E. (2011). How to design a winning business model. *Harvard Business Review, 89*(1/2), 100–107.

Chesbrough, H. (2006). *Open business models: How to thrive in the new innovation landscape.* Harvard Business Press.

Dane, E., & Pratt, M. G. (2007). Exploring intuition and its role in managerial decision making. *Academy of Management Review, 32*(1), 33–54.

Gassmann, H., Frankenberger, K., & Csik, M. (2014). *The business model navigator.* Pearson Education Limited.

Hill, L. C., Schilling, M. A., & Jones, G. R. (2016). *Strategic management theory: An integrated approach.* Cengage Learning.

IKEA. (2024). Retrieved March 28, 2024, from https://t.ly/PYHhb

Johnson, M. W. (2010). *Seizing the white space: Business model innovation for growth and renewal.* Harvard Business Press.

Kudina, A., Yip, G. S., & Barkema, H. G. (2008). Born global. *Business Strategy Review, 19*(4), 38–44.

Linder, J., & Cantrell, S. (2000). *Changing business models: Surveying the landscape.* Accenture Institute for Strategic Change.

Osterwalder, A., & Pigneur, Y. (2010). *Business model generation: A handbook for visionaries, game changers, and challengers.* John Wiley and Sons.

Petersen, B., & Welch, L. S. (2003). International business development and the internet, post-hype. *Management International Review, 43*(1), 7–29.

Root, F. (1994). *Entry strategies for international markets.* Lexington Books.

Root, F. R. (1998). *Entry strategies for international markets.* John Wiley & Sons.

Taran, Y., Nielsen, C., Montemari, M., Thomsen, P., & Paolone, F. (2016). Business model configurations: A five-V framework to map out potential innovation routes. *European Journal of Innovation Management, 19*(4), 492–527.

Teece, D. J., & Pisano, G. (1987). *Collaborative arrangements and technology strategy.* School of Business Administration, University of California.

Timmers, P. (1998). Business models for electronic markets. *Electronic Markets, 8*(2), 3–8.

Welch, L. S., & Luostarinen, R. (1988). Internationalization: Evolution of a concept. *Journal of General Management, 14*(2), 34–55.

CHAPTER 8

Toward an IB-BM Research Program

> *To see a World in a Grain of Sand*
> *And a Heaven in a Wild Flower,*
> *Hold Infinity in the palm of your hand*
> *And Eternity in an hour.*
> —William Blake

8.1 Captain's Log

Much can be learned about the voyages of a ship from its captain's log—navigation, operation, safety, compliance, decisions made and followed—especially during critical events, whether sailing in calm or turbulent waters. Although the captain's log of the *Titanic* was never recovered, a reconstruction of the hours before it sank reveals a series of decisions and circumstances that "sealed its fate." *Inter alia*, it was "a tragic chain of errors on the part of the well-meaning crew, the pernicious influence of the ship's haughty owner, who was aboard for the maiden trip, and a fatal overconfidence in the infallibility of early twentieth-century technology,"[1] misreading the environment, and ignoring the warning signals that led to sinking of the *Titanic*.

Switching contexts from the *Titanic* to one in which a firm, say, ceased trading following a withdrawal from its international markets and activities, the above reasons for "failure" can be valid, easily applied to explain and understand this firm cross-border organizational gestalt—pattern, capacity, and logic—that led to its total de-internationalization. A successful navigation between these three, cross-border, voyages—internationalization, de-internationalization, and re-internationalization—we conjecture is dependent on BMI (Fig. 1.1), which can assist the "captain" with mapping and outlining, for example, current and intended offerings portfolio (value proposition), target segments (value segment), operation plan and costs (value configurations), business partner collaborations (value network), and revenue stream (value capture). We also conjecture that a successful "voyage" or international growth of a firm, navigating and adapting in a VUCA world, reflecting on and responding to a plethora of opportunities and threats, are dependent on a symbiosis of cross-border organizational gestalt and BMI. The IB-BM research program that we put forward below is founded on the promising potential of the symbiosis between these two research streams.

8.2 Substantive (Inter)disciplinary Contributions

During our "voyage" toward the IB-BM research program that we discuss below we have refined existing and built new (inter)disciplinary knowledge. From the theory of the firm perspective, we suggest a firm can develop and pursue two types of organizational gestalt: domestic and cross-border or international. We further maintain that *organizational gestalt* consists of *pattern, capacity,* and *logic*. A firm crossing national borders would design and implement a *cross-border gestalt* based, for example, on a specific *internationalization* pattern, capacity, and logic. A firm that de-internationalizes or re-internationalizes would develop and pursue respective de-internationalization or re-internationalization gestalt consisting of respective *de-internationalization or re-internationalization* patterns, capacities, and logics. From a business model perspective, we define *business model innovation* as "a process of reconfiguring organizational gestalt of the firm."

From the IB theory perspective, we advocate for a *holistic view of cross-border or international business activity of the firm* by positioning "internationalization, de-internationalization, and re-internationalization" as part of the "cross-border activity" of the firm. We further define these three types of cross-border activity. *Internationalization* is defined as "a process and a state that allow firms to gradually or instantly cross national borders to commit to diverse relationships with key stakeholders in international contexts." *De-internationalization* is "the firm's capacity to reconfigure its organizational gestalt before or at the real point of no return." *Re-internationalization* is "a process and a state that allow a firm to reconfigure its pattern, capacity, and logic to gradually or instantly cross national borders following total or partial de-internationalization."

As re-internationalization is a less-studied and understood phenomenon, compared to internationalization and de-internationalization, we engaged in theorizing and theory building to conceptualize re-internationalization. In addition to the above, newly advanced definition of re-internationalization, we developed a *typology of re-internationalization* (Fig. 4.2) and its four types—imitating, balancing, rejuvenating, and taking time-off—by cross-tabulating successful and unsuccessful dimensions of internationalization and de-internationalization. We defined *re-internationalization errors*, i.e., errors of commission (Re-e1) and errors of omission (Re-e2), that allow firms to understand the timing of and commitment to re-internationalization.

Building on the *central, interdisciplinary conjecture of the book* that the relationship between de-internationalization and re-internationalization is best understood, theoretically and empirically, through the moderating effect of BMI, we developed a *de-internationalization, re-internationalization, and BMI intersection framework* (Fig. 1.2). We employed this framework to explore the relationship between the "hows" and "whys" of de-internationalization and BMI (Tables 6.1 and 6.2) and the "hows" of re-internationalization and BMI (Table 7.1). Drawing on these interdisciplinary conceptualizations, we built a *framework*, a *middle-range theory*,[2] of the relationship between de-internationalization and re-internationalization, moderated by BMI (Table 7.3). We see this framework as a subset of the IB-BM research program that we discuss in the next section.

8.3 Toward an IB-BM Research Program

8.3.1 IB-BM Research Program Framework

Research programs are essential for generating and advancing new, interdisciplinary knowledge and research fields.[3] Drawing on extant research programs,[4] we put forward an IB-BM research program founded on the following key elements: "a set of substantive [theoretical] and methodological working strategies; a network of interrelated unit theories [and methodologies] embodying these strategies; and a set of theory-based [and empirical-based] models applying these theories [and methodologies] to concrete instances."[5] Inspired by these key elements of a research program, we put forward a framework to guide the IB-BMI research program. We built the framework by cross-tabulating the cross-border activity gestalt of a firm and BM value drivers (Fig. 8.1).

Our framework is based on the extended application of the initial conjecture we set for this book. Herein we conjecture that BMI moderates gestalts or the elements of a gestalt across and within a cross-border activity of the firm. Figure 1.2 and Table 7.3 are examples of the former; Fig. 8.1 provides an example of the latter. An intersection in Fig. 8.1 of a gestalt element and a BM value driver defines a potential research theme (RT) that can be problematized, conceptualized, and studied. At least 45 potential RTs (RT1, RT2, RT3, ..., RTn) can be pursued independently within the IB-BMI research program from theoretical, methodological, and empirical perspectives (Fig. 8.1).

It can be observed (and expected) that the IB-BM research program will start with a network of *substantive* and *interdisciplinary* theories and methodologies from IB and BM research fields and their respective *working* theoretical and methodological strategies. In the process, the aim is to grow this network into *interrelated* theories and methodologies by developing *theory-driven* and *empirical-driven* frameworks and models, then

		Cross-border gestalt							
		Internationalization gestalt			De-internationalization gestalt			Re-internationalization gestalt		
		P_i	C_i	L_i	$P_{de\text{-}i}$	$C_{de\text{-}i}$	$L_{de\text{-}i}$	$P_{re\text{-}i}$	$C_{re\text{-}i}$	$L_{re\text{-}i}$
Business Model Drivers	Value proposition	RT1	RT2	RT3	...	...	...	...	...	...
	Value segment	...	...	...	...	...	...	...	...	...
	Value configuration	...	...	...	...	...	...	...	...	...
	Value network	...	...	...	...	...	...	...	...	...
	Value capture	...	...	...	...	...	...	...	...	RTn

Fig. 8.1 IB-BM research program framework

applying them to concrete conceptual and empirical interdisciplinary cases. We do hope this will encourage researchers to see the IB-BMI research program as "involving a choice between modes of engagement entailing different relationships between theory and method, concept and object, and researcher and researched."[6] In this book, we engaged solely in interdisciplinary theory building and theorizing (Chaps. 6 and 7) to illustrate how IB and BMI concepts can be intersected, and their relationship conceptualized. Researchers will have to develop and adopt research program methodological guidelines to study the IB-BM intersection. An example of basic methodological decisions and steps may pertain to: "(1) sample selection, (2) real-time process observation, (3) selecting core concepts for observing [IB-BMI] processes, (4) identifying and comparing alternative models to explain observed processes, and (5) addressing problems of measurements and sequence analysis to test alternative process models."[7] In the early stage of the IB-BM program, researchers may pursue theory-data-context iteration and consilience of inductions[8] to develop substantive, interdisciplinary, interrelated, and transcendent theory- and practitioner-based applied frameworks.

8.3.2 IB-BM Research Sub-Programs

At the same time, the IB-BM research program can be divided into vertical and horizontal sub-programs: cross-border (internationalization, de-internationalization, and re-internationalization) and BM (value proposition, value segment, value configuration, value network, and value capture), respectively. An example of a "vertical" sub-program, a re-internationalization sub-program and its respective exemplary research questions, is presented in Fig. 8.2.

Several theoretical and practical implications can be envisaged by the end of such a sub-program. For example, this sub-program framework (Fig. 8.2) can help identify and address the following fine-grained research questions. To what extent are firms' decision-makers familiar with the reasons leading to re-internationalization and business model configurations available to them? To what extent do (can) they experiment with opportunities to enable re-internationalization and new business model configurations? How to avoid being trapped in their dominant logic and help them "open the blinders" regarding dominant logic and avoid or minimize the prospects of failure. The findings from this sub-program will allow researchers to better understand the complexity of the IB-BM intersection and, eventually, the cross-border activity of the firm.

Value Drivers	Re-internationalization gestalt		
	P_{re-i}	C_{re-i}	L_{re-i}
Value Proposition	How firms adapt their offering portfolios when re-internationalizing	What resources and capabilities are needed to successfully effect re-internationalization offering portfolio	How firms align their re-internationalization offering portfolios to the new cross-border strategy
Value Segment	How firms find new and/or re-target existing customer segments to re-internationalize	What resource and capability configuration best supports new and/or revised international customer segments	What are the strategic reasons behind the firm's decision to target new or re-target existing customer segments
Value Configuration	How errors of commission (Re-e1) and omission (Re-e2) affect the choice and timing of re-entry modes	How firms reconfigure their BMs, resources and operations to successfully re-interna onalize	How re-configuration of resources and capabilities to support re-internationalization are aligned to the firm's long-term objectives
Value Network	How existing and/or new partnerships support re-internationalization pace and timing	How imitating or rejuvenating affect the choice and scope of partnership to re-internationalize	How partnership goals align with the firm's re-internationalization strategy
Value Capture	How firms design their international pricing mix and value capture mechanisms when re-internationalizing	How firms optimize their capacity to ensure effective value capture during re-internationalization	How firms align their re-internationalization value capture strategy with the firms' overall growth objectives

Fig. 8.2 A re-internationalization sub-program: An example

From a practical viewpoint, such a sub-program could be viewed as a practical strategic learning toolkit available to inspire firms toward different re-internationalization avenues they can pursue to revive their cross-border activities and, eventually, boost their international growth. By identifying a respective re-internationalization path, practitioners could avoid the trap of dominant logic, gain inspiration regarding how to deal with re-internationalization, learn from it, and reconfigure the firms' future re-internationalization growth strategies. As a result, the availability of a wide range of business model configurations allows decision-makers to consider many re-internationalization alternatives, each with its new or revised degree of risk, costs, resources, and market commitment.

8.3.3 A multidimensional and Multilevel Research Program

In addition to its international and interdisciplinary nature, the IB-BMI research program will be inter-technological and inter-sectorial; it will be a *quadruple-i*—international, interdisciplinary, inter-technological and inter-sectoral[9]—research program. This points to diverse contexts and levels of analysis where the IB-BM intersection could be studied. This can be achieved, for example, by *zooming-in* on *micro-level* or firm-level operating processes, *zooming-out* on *meso-* or *macro-level* factors and processes, *iterating* between zooming-in and zooming-out, and *abstracting* or *theorizing* during the zooming-in and zooming-out iterations within and across micro, meso, and macro levels, abstracting/theorizing from the operational level to the highest level of abstraction, IB-BMI narratives, or to the first level of abstraction, IB-BM configurations.

An example of a framework that can guide IB-BM researchers to study the BM-BM intersection within and across diverse levels and contexts is presented in Fig. 8.3. Within each level, we conjecture academics and practitioners will engage in abstracting or theorizing the firm, its embeddedness with new or existing structures at meso and macro levels. We also conjecture that the weight each value driver has during iterating, abstracting, and theorizing will vary across the micro, meso, and macro levels.

			Cross-border gestalt							
			Internationalization gestalt			*De-internationalization gestalt*			*Re-internationalization gestalt*		
			P_i	C_i	L_i	P_{de-i}	C_{de-i}	L_{de-i}	P_{re-i}	C_{re-i}	L_{re-i}
Iterating	Zooming-in	Micro	Abstracting/theorizing: 5V-framework; BM configurations; operating business processes; meta-models								
	Zooming-out	Meso	Abstracting/theorizing: 5V-framework; eco-system BM; substantive graphical frameworks								
		Macro	Abstracting/theorizing: 5V-framework; ontological graphical frameworks; architypes; narratives								

Fig. 8.3 Researching IB-BM intersection at micro, meso, and macro levels

8.4 An Exciting "voyage" Ahead

One of the biggest challenges, if not the biggest, that IB-BM researchers must overcome is the *alienation* between the two cultures,[10] IB and BM; their lack of *consilience*.[11] Can they "talk" to each other? Can they "jump together?" After all, they have diverse and divergent research strategy logics defined by respective constitutive assumptions (paradigms), epistemological stances (metaphors), and favored methodologies (puzzle solving).[12] These challenges are amplified by their contrasting domain definitions.[13]

Despite the complexity of the IB-BM intersection and challenges that lie ahead, we believe future research at the intersection of these two research streams and cultures will contribute to a better understanding of firms' currently under-researched, nonlinear cross-border activities. We also believe this IB-BM research program will have an impact on practice by leading to a better understanding of how firms can reconfigure or reinvent their business models during failure, growth, decline, or (strategic) departure from what is normal or expected. Such an embryonic research program will undoubtedly create more questions than answers, making it an exciting, thought-provoking avenue for future research and practice pondering in a VUCA world.

Notes

1. Brown (2003).
2. A middle range theory lies "between the minor but necessary working hypothesis that evolve in abundance during day-to-day research and the all-inclusive systematic efforts to develop a unified theory that will explain all the observed uniformities of social behavior, social organization, and social change" (Merton 1996, p. 41).
3. Berger and Zelditch (2002).
4. Berger and Zelditch (1998), Van de Ven and Huber (1990), Van de Ven and Poole (1990), Wagner and Berger (2002).
5. Berger et al. (2005, p. 132).
6. Morgan (1983, p. 19).
7. Van de Ven and Poole (1990, p. 316).
8. Whewell (1845).
9. LNETN (2024).
10. Snow (1962).

11. Wilson (1998).
12. Morgan (1983).
13. For example, the IB domain is defined by (http://www.palgrave.com/gp/journal/41267):

    - activities, strategies, structures, and decision-making processes of multinational enterprises
    - interactions between multinational enterprises and other actors, organizations, institutions, and markets
    - the cross-border activities of firms (e.g., intrafirm trade, finance, investment, technology transfers, offshore services)
    - how the international environment (e.g., cultural, economic, legal, political) affects the activities, strategies, structures and decision-making processes of firms
    - the international dimensions of organizational forms (e.g., strategic alliances, mergers and acquisitions) and activities (e.g., entrepreneurship, knowledge-based competition, corporate governance)
    - cross-country comparative studies of businesses, business processes and organizational behavior in different countries and environments
    - industry 4.0 in IB (e.g., the profound effects that 4.0 technologies have on the governance, the strategies, the structures, and the organizational functioning of internationally operating firms)
    - global sustainability (e.g., how ESGD performance indicators, environmental and climate change impact mitigation, and a variety of dimensions of distributional justice—the equity, diversity and inclusion movements throughout the world—affect the functioning of internationally operating firms)

    The BM domain is defined by (https://journals.aau.dk/index.php/JOBM/about):

    - business model design: designing, rejuvenating, innovating and facilitating
    - implementing business models: the execution process
    - commercialization and exploitation of ideas through business models: challenging entrepreneurial processes
    - seeking the true benefits of a globalized world: how internationalization of activities affects business models
    - business model archetypes and key components: integrating building blocks and typologies

- the strategic partnerships of business models: roles and relationships within and among business models
- business models and high-tech ventures
- the performance of business models: dilemmas and paradoxes of performance measurement consequences
- defining what business models are about: the epistemological and conceptual roots of business models and their differences with strategy, strategic management, organization and business planning
- tools and techniques

REFERENCES

Berger, J., & Zelditch, Jr, M. (Eds.). (1998). *Status, power, and legitimacy: Strategies and theories.* Transaction Publishers.

Berger, J., & Zelditch, M. (Eds.). (2002). *New directions in contemporary sociological theory.* Rowman & Littlefield.

Berger, A. N., Miller, N. H., Petersen, M. A., Rajan, R. G., & Stein, J. C. (2005). Does function follow organizational form? Evidence from the lending practices of large and small banks. *Journal of Financial economics, 76*(2), 237–269.

Brown, D. G. (2003). *The last log of the titanic.* International Marine/Ragged Mountain Press

LNETN (2024). Legitimation of newness and its impact on EU agenda for change. https://t.ly/4Wc32

Merton, R. K. (1996). *On social structure and science.* University of Chicago Press.

Morgan, G. (1983). More on metaphor: Why we cannot control tropes in administrative science. *Administrative Science Quarterly, 28*(4), 601–607.

Snow, C. P. (1962). *The two cultures and the scientific revolution.* Cambridge: Cambridge University Press.

Van de Ven, A. H., & Huber, G. P. (1990). Longitudinal field research methods for studying processes of organizational change. *Organization Science, 1*(3), 213–219.

Van de Ven, A. H., & Poole, M. S. (1990). Methods for studying innovation development in the Minnesota Innovation Research Program. *Organization Science, 1*(3), 313–335.

Wagner, D. G., & Berger, J. (2002). Expectation states theory: An evolving research program. *New Directions in Contemporary Sociological Theory, 41*, 5–22.

Whewell, W. (1845). *The philosophy of inductive sciences.* John W. Parker: London.

Wilson, E. O. (1998). *Consilience: The unity of knowledge.* Knopf.

Index[1]

A

Abstraction/abstracting, 7, 76–78, 80, 81n31, 82n35, 82n36, 99, 123
Acquisition, 2, 14, 15, 17, 36, 40, 59, 64, 74, 97, 125n13

B

Backshoring, 37
Balancing, 7, 67, 92, 115, 119
Blinds/blinders, 18, 32, 33, 72, 78, 87
Born global, 15, 16, 105
Brownfield investments, 2, 14
Business model(BM), ix–xi, 3, 5–8, 16, 33, 54–57, 59, 61, 71–80, 80n5, 81n8, 82n35, 82n38, 82n40, 89–99, 103, 104, 106–114, 117–124, 125–126n13

business model value drivers, 7, 8, 45n39, 78, 88–99, 103, 104, 106–112, 114, 115, 120
Business model configurations, 13, 79, 121, 122
The 5-V framework, 7, 8, 78–79, 88, 89
Business model innovation (BMI)
  garage firms, 75
  network-level BMI, 7, 75
  open BMI, 7, 74
  open, inside-out BMI, 74
  open, inside-out/outside-in BMI, 75
  open, outside-in BMI, 74
  Semi-Closed BMI, 74
  spin-offs firms, 75
Business model innovation lenses, x, 99, 115
Business model innovation types, 7, 72–74, 80, 81n8, 104–105, 108

[1] Note: Page numbers followed by 'n' refer to notes.

C

Capabilities, 1, 2, 14, 36, 56, 57, 59, 62, 63, 76, 89, 96, 100n17, 103, 104
Capacity, 2, 6–8, 9n34, 14–16, 18, 19, 31, 33, 62, 63, 65, 66, 72, 76, 87, 96, 97, 99, 103, 104, 115, 118, 119
Cocooning, 33, 55, 56
Commitment, 5, 6, 14, 15, 18, 19, 21n47, 30–34, 36, 37, 44, 57, 61, 62, 66, 109, 119, 122
Context, viii, 5, 6, 14, 19, 33, 38, 40, 44, 97, 98, 117, 119, 123
Contracting out, 38
Critical events, 16, 38, 40, 44, 64, 65, 87, 117
Cross-border activities, x, 2–4, 6, 9n34, 13, 18, 19, 21n47, 28–30, 40, 54, 62–64, 66, 80, 87, 103, 118, 120–122, 124, 125n13

D

Decision makers, 2, 5, 7, 14, 18, 30, 32, 40, 44, 64, 76–78, 80, 92, 94, 111, 114, 121, 122
Decoupling, 37, 89
De-export, 38
De-franchise, 38
De-internationalization
  definition, 28–29
  external factors, 36, 59, 77
  hows of de-internationalization, 36–38, 89–92
  internal factors, 35, 36
  modes of de-internationalization, 38
  point of no return, 5, 6, 33, 37, 57, 65, 119
  reasons to de-internationalize, 5, 31, 96
  typology of de-internationalization, 34
  whys of de-internationalization, 7, 8, 35–36, 40, 89, 92–98, 103, 112, 115, 119

E

Entrapment, 7, 18, 32, 71, 72, 78
Entry modes (modes of entry), 14–16, 18, 36–38, 63, 66, 104–105, 108, 109
Error of commission, 6, 7, 32, 56, 57, 62, 64, 65, 67, 99, 115
Error of correction, 31, 32, 56
Error of omission, 6, 7, 32, 33, 56, 57, 62, 65–67, 99, 115
Exit modes, 8, 37, 92, 99
Exporting, 2, 5, 14, 15, 34, 38, 59, 63, 76, 107, 108

F

Foreign market entry modes, 14, 15, 18, 104, 107
Franchising, 2, 14, 38, 80, 88, 108–110
Friend-shoring, 37

G

Gestalt
  de-internationalization gestalt, 80, 99
  firm gestalt, 6, 16, 18, 19, 33, 44, 54, 62, 64–66, 71, 72, 80, 87, 88, 118–120
  internationalization gestalt, 8, 19, 65, 66, 76, 80
  organizational gestalt, 6, 7, 9n34, 16, 18, 19, 33, 44, 62, 71, 72, 80, 118, 119

re-internationalization gestalt, 63, 66, 80, 115, 118
Greenfield investments, 36, 41, 104, 110

I

Imitating, 7, 65–67, 115, 119
Importing, 38
Indirect exporting, 34, 38
Innovation, vii, ix, x, 1–3, 29, 36, 71–80, 81n7, 81n8, 89, 97, 100n17, 118
International business–business model framework, 112–115
International business–business model research program, x, xi, 8, 117–124
Internationalization
 definition, 14, 19
 gradual internationalization, 14, 59
 instant internationalization, 16
 motives for internationalization, 40
Iterating, 7, 34, 77, 80, 99, 123

J

Joint ventures, 2, 14, 15, 18, 36, 38–40, 74–76, 88, 89, 92, 97, 107

L

Level of abstraction, 77, 78, 80, 123
Leverage buy-out, 38
Licensing, 2, 14, 16, 38, 75, 97, 108
Licensing in, 38, 74
Licensing out, 105
Logic, ix, 2, 5–7, 9n34, 16, 18, 19, 33, 54, 59, 62, 63, 65, 66, 71, 72, 76, 77, 87, 99, 103, 104, 115, 118, 119, 121, 122, 124

M

Macro-level, 77, 123
Merger, 74, 125n13
Meso level, 76, 77, 80, 81n31, 123
Micro level, 76, 77, 80, 81n31, 123
Multidimensional/multilevel research program, 123

N

Near-shoring, 37, 89

O

Off-shoring, 37, 89

P

Partial withdrawal, 7, 34, 38, 39, 54, 62, 89
Pattern, 1, 2, 7, 8, 9n34, 14, 15, 18, 19, 30, 40, 59, 62, 63, 65, 66, 72, 76, 82n40, 87, 99, 103, 104, 107, 115, 118, 119
Policy makers, 6, 8, 13, 27, 28, 38, 40
Policy making, 28, 30

R

Re-coupling, 37
Re-entry, 104–105
Re-internationalization
 definition, 7, 19, 54, 56, 61–63, 119
 external stimuli, 63, 64
 hows of re-internationalization, 8, 64–66, 103–105, 112, 115, 119
 internal stimuli, 63
 pattern, capacity and logic, 7, 9n34, 62, 63, 65, 66, 115, 119

Re-internationalization (*cont.*)
  typology of re-internationlization, 7, 66, 67, 119
  whys of re-internationalization, 8, 63–64, 106–112
Rejuvenating, 7, 67, 115, 119, 125n13
Research program, x, xi, 6, 8, 117–124
Re-shoring, 37

S
Selling out, 38
Spin-off, 38, 75
Strategic alliances, 14, 75, 92, 125n13
Supply chain, 39, 76, 88, 92, 106

T
Taking time-off, 7, 67, 115, 119
Terms and concepts, ix, 3, 6, 19, 34, 44n1, 61, 81n31, 89, 121
Time-out, 62
Timing, 2, 5, 14, 15, 18, 44, 56, 57, 62, 65, 119
Total withdrawal, 34, 35, 44, 57, 60, 62, 64, 99
Turning point, 32, 33

V
Value capture, x, 5, 7, 8, 80, 89, 92, 98, 111–112, 118, 121
Value configuration, x, 5, 7, 8, 76, 77, 79, 88, 89, 92, 96–97, 108, 118, 121
Value drivers, 5, 7, 8, 77, 88–99, 103, 104, 106–112, 114, 115, 120, 123
Value network, x, 5, 7, 8, 79, 80, 88, 89, 92, 97, 109–110, 118, 121
Value proposition, x, 5, 7, 8, 72, 78, 79, 82n40, 88, 89, 92, 94–96, 106, 118, 121
Value segment, x, 5, 7, 8, 78, 79, 88, 89, 92, 95, 96, 106–108, 118, 121
Velocity, 57, 62, 63, 65
Volatile, uncertain, complex, and ambiguous (VUCA), 1–3, 8, 81n8, 118, 124

Z
Zooming In, 7, 62, 63, 75–77, 80, 81n31, 99, 123
Zooming Out, 7, 62, 75–77, 80, 81n31, 99, 123

GPSR Compliance

The European Union's (EU) General Product Safety Regulation (GPSR) is a set of rules that requires consumer products to be safe and our obligations to ensure this.

If you have any concerns about our products, you can contact us on ProductSafety@springernature.com

In case Publisher is established outside the EU, the EU authorized representative is:

Springer Nature Customer Service Center GmbH
Europaplatz 3
69115 Heidelberg, Germany

Batch number: 08758204

Printed by Printforce, the Netherlands